ROUTLEDGE LIBRARY EDITIONS: WW2

Volume 29

SCRAP BOOK OF THE WORKING MEN'S COLLEGE IN TWO WORLD WARS

SCRAP BOOK OF THE WORKING MEN'S COLLEGE IN TWO WORLD WARS

Edited by
MURIEL FRANKLIN

LONDON AND NEW YORK

This edition first published in 2022
by Routledge
2 Park Square, Milton Park, Abingdon, Oxon OX14 4RN

and by Routledge
605 Third Avenue, New York, NY 10158

Routledge is an imprint of the Taylor & Francis Group, an informa business

First published privately in 1965 by Routledge & Kegan Paul

All rights reserved. No part of this book may be reprinted or reproduced or utilised in any form or by any electronic, mechanical, or other means, now known or hereafter invented, including photocopying and recording, or in any information storage or retrieval system, without permission in writing from the publishers.

Trademark notice: Product or corporate names may be trademarks or registered trademarks, and are used only for identification and explanation without intent to infringe.

British Library Cataloguing in Publication Data
A catalogue record for this book is available from the British Library

ISBN: 978-1-03-201217-9 (Set)
ISBN: 978-1-00-319367-8 (Set) (ebk)
ISBN: 978-1-03-208048-2 (Volume 29) (hbk)
ISBN: 978-1-03-208049-9 (Volume 29) (pbk)
ISBN: 978-1-00-321267-6 (Volume 29) (ebk)

DOI: 10.4324/9781003212676

Publisher's Note
The publisher has gone to great lengths to ensure the quality of this reprint but points out that some imperfections in the original copies may be apparent.

Disclaimer
The publisher has made every effort to trace copyright holders and would welcome correspondence from those they have been unable to trace.

Scrap Book of
THE WORKING MEN'S COLLEGE
in Two World Wars

━━━━━━━━━━━━━━━

MADE BY MURIEL FRANKLIN

LONDON
ROUTLEDGE & KEGAN PAUL

*Published privately in 1965
by Routledge and Kegan Paul Ltd
Broadway House, 68–74 Carter Lane
London, E.C.4*

CONTENTS

LIST OF ILLUSTRATIONS vii
DEDICATION viii
ACKNOWLEDGEMENTS ix
PREFACE – THE COLLEGE xi

Part One

I GENERAL PICTURE – 1914   3
II WORKING MEN'S COLLEGE – 1914, *by A. J. W. Walker*   7
III SOME IMPORTANT PEOPLE AND A HERO IN THE COLLEGE   11
IV WORK PARTIES AND MARKS FELLOWSHIP   15
V ON THE WAR – STUDENT TEACHER MEETINGS   18
VI FOUNDERS' NIGHTS AND OTHER COLLEGE OCCASIONS   25
VII JOTTINGS FROM THE JOURNAL   32
VIII OLD STUDENTS' SUPPERS AND TEAS 1914/18   37
IX LETTERS FROM THE HOME FRONT   47
X SOME LETTERS FROM THE ROYAL NAVY   50
XI LETTERS FROM THE B.E.F., FRANCE   56
XII MORE LETTERS FROM THE B.E.F., FRANCE   64
XIII LETTERS FROM MANY THEATRES OF WAR – EUROPE TO THE FAR EAST   73
XIV THE END OF AN ERA   84

CONTENTS

Part Two

	ELLIS FRANKLIN *by Vera Deacon*	89
XV	INTRODUCTION	91
XVI	EXTRACTS FROM THE JOURNAL IN THE EARLY DAYS OF THE WAR	95
XVII	THE COLLEGE AT WAR	101
XVIII	THE COLLEGE AND THE SECOND WORLD WAR *by the Vice-Principal, F. Gahan*	109
XIX	WAR WORK PARTY, 1939	114
XX	THE PLAYING FIELD DURING THE WAR	122
XXI	DUDLEY GILL TAKES A LOOK AT THE COLLEGE	126
XXII	COLLEGE PERSONALITIES	129
XXIII	"NO MEMORIAL..."	133
XXIV	MORE NOTES FROM THE JOURNAL	137
XXV	COLLEGE COUNCIL AND EMERGENCY COMMITTEE REPORTS	144
XXVI	WAR EMERGENCY COMMITTEE REPORT	153
XXVII	OLD STUDENTS' CLUB ANNUAL FUNCTIONS, 1939–45	157
XXVIII	LETTERS FROM THE HOME FRONT – CIVIL AND MILITARY	163
XXIX	LETTERS FROM THE ROYAL NAVY	171
XXX	LETTERS FROM EUROPEAN THEATRES OF WAR	185
XXXI	LETTERS FROM THE MIDDLE EAST AND CENTRAL MEDITERRANEAN FORCES	193
XXXII	LETTERS FROM AFRICA, CANADA AND GERMANY	203
XXXIII	'THANK YOU' CONCERT AND RECEPTION TO THE LADIES OF THE WORK PARTY – 1946. ENVOI	215

ILLUSTRATIONS

Ellis A. Franklin	*Frontispiece*
Sir Charles Lucas, k.c.b., k.c.m.g.	*facing page* 10
Arthur S. Lupton	11
Corporal Christie, v.c. (*Soldier, 1914–18*)	76
Bill Walder, (*Soldier, 1939–45*)	76
Frank Gahan	108
George Bankes	109
Major-General Sir F. B. Maurice, k.c.m.g., c.b., d.litt., ll.d.	128
The Right Hon. Lord Greene	129

To the memory of Ellis Franklin, who loved the College, and laboured for its good for over forty-five years, this work is fondly dedicated by his wife.

ACKNOWLEDGEMENTS

IT is in memory of my husband that I have made and am giving this book to the Working Men's College, that stood for so much in his life, and to which he gave so much of his time, his thought, his energy and his strength.

I have been helped throughout in selecting and copying the letters by Vera Deacon, whose husband, George, now honorary librarian and College Fellow, and a member of the Executive Committee was, during the Second World War, at the receiving end of the Ladies War Work Party activities. Clare Gill, wife of Dudley who became Superintendent of the College in 1942, began the work with us, but illness unhappily intervened, and she was unable to continue.

To both these friends I want to express my grateful thanks for the assistance so readily given.

I am also indebted to Vera for undertaking the thankless, laborious, and unspectacular, but essential and valuable task, of making the first typescript of the book.

Without her help and criticism, and the practical, and critical interest of my son, Colin (of Messrs Routledge and Kegan Paul), who has also given much needed expert advice and assistance on the printing and production of the book, it could never have been completed.

I desire also to thank F. Gahan, A. J. Walker and Dudley Gill for their chapters on aspects of College life seen from inside in each period. They were active in the College at the relevant times, and write, to the great benefit of the book, of a scene of which they had a particular knowledge.

M. Franklin.

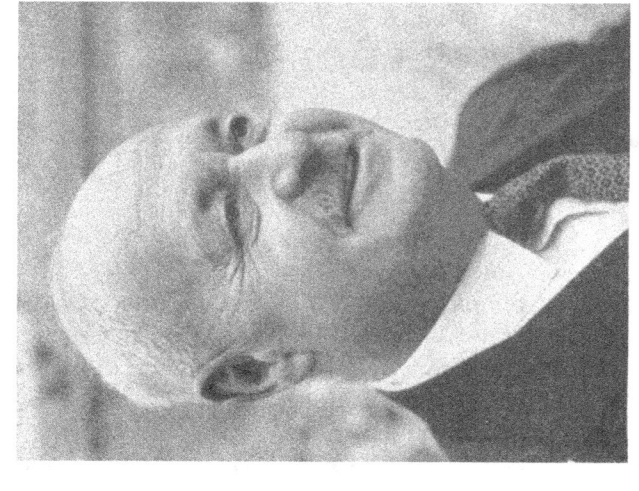

ELLIS A. FRANKLIN, O.B.E.
Vice-Principal 1922–29, Bursar 1931–48
Chairman Old Students' Club 1963–64

ELLIS A. FRANKLIN
10th K.O.Y.L.I. 1914–18

PREFACE—THE COLLEGE

THIS is a College book; but one hopes it may also be read by some who are outside the magic circle of that unique institution.

The intangibles of the College, which are its very life, are something that an outsider often finds it hard to understand.

The basic principle laid down by the founders in 1854 when they spoke of 'men of the working-classes and men from the universities meeting together for the common purpose of teaching and learning' strikes at the root of the matter.

The sharp class distinctions of those early days have mercifully been blunted, but the principle of mutual giving and receiving between men with different educational backgrounds and opportunities remains. The 'do-gooder' has no place in the College. Any teacher coming with that idea has to give up, or to conform to the far more worth while pattern of 'teaching and learning'. Deliberately, or because he is drawn into it, he must become a true 'common-room man'. As one of the correspondents quoted in this book wisely remarks, 'the common-room is a great leveller.'

The College was founded by a clergyman, but men of all religious denominations or of no religion, find the same welcome within its walls. The colour of your skin may be white, black or khaki, it is of no concern to anyone else; once you become a member of the College you are accepted on your merits alone. When on the occasion of the centenary celebrations Her Majesty the Queen and His Royal Highness the Duke of

PREFACE – THE COLLEGE

Edinburgh visited the College, even on such a brief look round the Duke observed, and commented on this true, effortless 'integration'.

The College spirit, compounded of so many elements – tolerance, loyalty and forebearance, the readiness to stand together in time of trouble, all come into it – is at the heart of the place. It has inspired men in the fighting services in two great wars to write from the farthest corners of the earth with nostalgic longing to the College, and drawn them as a magnet to itself on their brief periods of home leave, if only for a few hours. And after the wars it has brought them together again within its walls with the old loyalties reinforced, and the quiet sense of returning 'home'.

The College was founded when the educational opportunities for the poorer classes of an acutely class-conscious society were virtually non-existent. Longer school education, and the proliferation of adult institutes and evening classes in modern times has multiplied the opportunities for learning for all classes of men, and to that extent creates a new situation, that is also a challenge, for the College.

But a challenge it is well equipped to meet. Not only does it offer something unique within itself, but the unlimited freedom to embark on bold educational experiment, a fruit of the financial independence hard won between the wars, and a legitimate cause for pride, is a privilege denied to council subsidized institutions. And as long as men are willing to serve the College selflessly, to shoulder responsibility on its behalf, and to help one another; as long as tolerance, the friendliness of the common-room and the 'common bond of teaching and learning' between teacher and student remain its watchword, the old loyalties and affections that under its aegis throughout the years have bound men of different backgrounds in friendship together, the 'College spirit', that great intangible, will survive.

But if the spirit of service without material reward dies, either from policy or indifference, all that is best and unique in the College dies too.

In its Crowndale Road building the College has survived two world wars without ever closing its doors. But the picture in 1914 differs in many respects from that of 1939.

PREFACE – THE COLLEGE

It occurred to me that a scrap book giving a thumb-nail sketch of the state of affairs in Crowndale Road, and of the thoughts and reactions within the College circle, in each of these two very different periods, could be of interest to future generations of College men; and that the most satisfactory way to do this would be not only to describe from contemporary accounts the life in the College itself, but to reprint a selection of the letters received from College men – mainly from the fighting services – in each period. It seemed to me that such accounts would help to fill out and enliven the picture, and bring into sharper focus the points of view and ideals not only of the years of the Second World War that are closer to men's memories, but of that earlier period, when, like a thunderbolt out of a clear sky, universal war fell suddenly on a seemingly secure and peaceful land.

Certain contrasts in attitude and personal relationships in the two periods are apparent in the letters.

There is, in the earlier correspondence, a deference shown towards those holding high office in the College, that would be out of place today. Almost the only easy intimate letters are those sent from one College student to another, or to Pocock, later to become Bursar, but in 1914 the Chairman of the Marks Fellowship.

A further contrast with modern custom would seem to be the subject matter of the writer's inhibitions. While nothing from drains to lavatories or sex would cause embarrassment in modern times, the kind of emotionalism and virtuous highmindedness freely expressed in the early letters, natural and acceptable enough then, would condemn the writer and provoke ridicule today.

The hardships of war do not alter, except, perhaps, in form; the fundamentals of fed-upness, patriotic feeling, homesickness, remain unchanged. But the manner of their expression in the two wars was, in many ways, so different.

Searching through the files in the muniment room, and through old numbers of the *Journal* to dig out the material for this book, is like peering into a room through the panes of a bow window, seeing it from varying angles, each of which gives a different view and a different impression of what is there, though in truth the room remains unchanged.

PREFACE — THE COLLEGE

All the accounts in this volume are 'live', none based on hearsay. Though they show contrasts in attitudes and ways of thought and expression in the two periods, through it all, unchanged throughout the years, runs one consistent thread – loyalty to, and love for the College.

M. Franklin

PART ONE

1914

I

GENERAL PICTURE – 1914

THERE were some aspects of the First World War that in retrospect make one think of playing at soldiers. It had a romantic aura, at least at its onset, that was like something left over from the days of chivalry, or the bravado and spirit of adventure of the days of the first Elizabeth.

To understand this it is necessary to take a look at the contemporary scene. An Englishman's home was still his 'castle'; in theory at least, inviolate. A glance at an atlas showed the red of the British Empire sprawling across three-quarters of the map of the world. Perhaps there was some arrogance, but certainly there was glory in defending such power.

But at home the life of the working-classes on the whole was drab; their wages allowed little for the pleasures of life, and even those who regarded themselves as comfortably off accepted without question an inferior status and standard of living. Yet, even allowing for all this they were, on the whole, better off than their opposite numbers in most foreign countries – a fact of which they were proudly aware.

Loyalties were strong, but ignorance was rife. Elementary education, only recently compulsory, was what its name implied. Children left school at fourteen and went out to work. The opportunities for self-betterment through evening classes were few. All this, by contrast, gave a certain tinsel glamour to the prospect of becoming a soldier. But there was also emotional involvement. First the horror of the Serajevo murders, followed

GENERAL PICTURE – 1914

by the savage attack on Belgium in defiance of treaty obligations – the 'scrap of paper' mentality and the cruelty were deeply shocking to men's minds. By their violence and unscrupulousness the Germans had instantly welded the peace-loving British nation into a vigorous instrument of war, fired by righteous emotion passionately felt.

Some of its manifestations were strange; as when a group of young women started handing white feathers to every young man in the street not wearing the King's uniform. A silver badge for officers on leave, to pin on the lapel of a civilian coat, was devised and issued for officers and all men invalided out from the services, to protect them from this nuisance. 'Other ranks' in the forces were not affected as it was compulsory for them at all times to wear uniform in the street.

Enlistment in 1914 was entirely voluntary, and acquired as a result a heroic aura. Immense coloured recruiting posters carried a portrait of Lord Kitchener pointing a fiercely admonitory finger, over the caption 'Your country needs YOU', whilst others showed an accusing infant at his father's knee demanding to know 'What did YOU do in the Great War, Daddy?'

In 1914 the superficial trappings of war still retained their glamour. The cavalry was a romantic fact, an epic in embryo. Only slowly through the years did they become mechanized. The German Uhlan rode into battle with his lance; the British trooper, trained to feed and water his horse before attending to his own needs, was an actual, gallant figure. Guns were limbered by teams of horses, much of the transport was horse- or mule-drawn. The aeroplanes of our pitifully inadequate Air Force had to be crated and shipped to France. Reconnaissances were made from gas-filled balloons – perfect targets for enemy guns.

The Expeditionary Force of 'old contemptibles' who stayed the German advance at Mons were heroes of the calibre of those historic figures of the Crimean War who gave their lives in the tragic charge of the Light Brigade.

This was the atmosphere in which ageing gentlemen like Sir Charles Lucas, and some of the young and unfit, satisfied something of their patriotic fervour by joining or organizing some para-military organization, such as the Government-sponsored

GENERAL PICTURE – 1914

National Guard, which was roughly comparable to the Civil Defence organization and Home Guard of the Second World War, or the less official but no less enthusiastic Volunteer Training Corps.

The *Journal* of December gives a report of a meeting held with the object of forming a 'company of Volunteers in the College'. The speeches and indeed the whole episode are typical of the spirit of that time, and of Lucas himself, who was clearly the force behind this effort.

A College Training Corps (From the Journal, *1915)*
'On December 21st, 1914, a meeting was held in the Common Room, presided over by the Principal, to form a company of a corps for training those members who are prevented by their age or other disabilities from joining the army or territorial forces . . .'

. . . Resolutions were passed 'that steps be taken to form a College company in connection with the Central Association of Volunteer Training Corps' and 'That an organizing committee be formed consisting of Messrs Duchesne (Superintendent of the College), G. A. Taylor, Crawley, A. E. Taylor, Hepburn, Nield and Starling . . .'

. . . Mr. H. R. Scott of the O.T.C.,* has kindly undertaken the command of the College company.

In a stirring speech, Sir Charles Lucas began by pointing out that 'all should go on active service who could possibly do so', and the force now proposed to be formed was not to be in substitution for, but to supplement the work of the more active units, and was intended to be affiliated to the Central Association of Volunteer Training Corps. 'We are convinced of the righteousness of our cause in this war. England could never have held up her head again if she had stood aloof from the fight for liberty. In the name of our College traditions,' he asked his hearers to 'help our country in every way we could . . .'

A gentleman representing the Central Association of Volunteer Training Corps, explained the objects and regulations of that body, and gave information concerning drills and accoutrements. Forty drills were a minimum. No attestation was re-

* Later Sir Harold Scott, Chief Commissioner of Police.

quired. The expense involved was very small. A Norfolk jacket of grey-green waterproof cloth with shoulder-straps and military cuffs would cost 10s., second-hand Martini-Henry rifles cost £2 10s. each. Complete equipment would include brown gaiters, cord breeches, and military cap to match jacket. Men over thirty-eight were eligible. Those under that age should have a sound and adequate reason for not joining the regular army. If their reasons were inadequate they could not continue in the corps. There would be no legal obligation for any such to join the regulars, but moral suasion would be recognized. A list of those under thirty-eight should be kept for reference.

College Volunteers, 1915 (*From the* Journal)
'A meeting of the squads drilling in the Gymnasium was held on Friday March 17th, when the recommendations of the committee were placed before the members. Consideration was given to corps under the Central Association carrying on in the immediate vicinity of the College. It was finally decided to offer a company section, or perhaps two sections (a half-company), to the Hampstead Volunteer Reserve.'

II

WORKING MEN'S COLLEGE – 1914

IN the summer of 1914 the College was a flourishing concern in all respects. The administration was in the hands of such able and well liked men as Sir Charles Lucas (Principal), Lionel Jacob and Arthur Lupton (Vice-Principal). The office staff consisted of the redoubtable Duchesne (Superintendent as he was then called) assisted by Flint and Barnett, both Ormond Street old-timers.* The student body still included some who remembered the Founders. The teachers, both active and reserve, formed a splendid corps of brilliant and distinguished men. Differences in religion, politics, nationality and social prestige counted for nothing – all were College men. The 'College spirit' (afterwards to become a joke)† was a reality. Altogether the institution was in a strong position to face the crisis of August 4th, 1914. When that crisis came, the College responded well, teachers and students, in an ever-memorable surge of patriotism, flocked to the colours; yet, curiously enough, the College appeared to carry on as usual. Naturally there was much reorganization and many replacements to be faced before the autumn session began. Here Duchesne, on whom the authorities leaned heavily, outshone himself in persuasion and tact, not to mention sheer hard work. A full programme was offered and carried into effect. New teachers

* The College had premises in Great Ormond Street before moving to the present building.

† But only briefly – it has survived both wars.

came and new students, but the College absorbed them all. A minor domestic disturbance was caused when the Maurice Hall was taken over as a recruiting station, but life in the common-room continued much as before. If anything the common-room became more used by the students. There was much to talk about and a heightened sense of solidarity. Men in uniform were a common sight and discussion over the war was rife. The spirit of members was overwhelmingly loyal. One or two hardened pacifists stuck to their colours, but their influence was slight. . . . As G. M. Trevelyan said about the Boer War period, the Working Men's College was about the only place in London where a man could speak his mind. One must not exaggerate this aspect of things – the College as a whole was deeply, almost too emotionally loyal and sound.

The clubs and societies functioned normally. New societies were formed and flourished. The College lectures were as popular as ever and were widely appreciated in the turmoil of contemporary war-time life. The Old Students' Club held their meetings regularly. It was at one of these that Sir Frederick Maurice made what was probably his first appearance at Crowndale Road. Another feature that carried on old traditions was the concerts in the Maurice Hall and the common-room. One of the most memorable of these was when Wetenhall, then on leave, entertained the audience with his own songs at the piano. Starling, C. H. Perry, Bob Hagarty, Dumbrill and a dozen other well-known College characters also performed at these concerts.

What of the men in the forces? Their letters were published in the *Journal* by the indefatigable Pocock – and their material needs were attended to by the Marks Fellowship. . . . Duchesne knew what every man was up to, and passed on information incessantly. The existence of the College was a great comfort to the fighting men. . . . 'Blighty' for most meant home *and* the W.M.C.

The actual number of men in the forces was considerable and the casualty list was correspondingly high. It was with constant dread that one watched the notice-board for names. The War Memorial Board in the entrance hall tells its own tale, and one knew personally nine out of ten of the students and teachers commemorated there.

WORKING MEN'S COLLEGE – 1914

Lest it be thought that the appalling record of casualties contrasts ill with the account of the concerts and similar activities that went on in the College, it should be remembered that 1914–18 was a 'gay war', thanks to the almost total absence of air attacks on the home front, and the official exhortation to carry on with 'business as usual'. The first thing a man did on leave was to go to 'a show'.

There were men helping to keep the College alive in those early days of war whose names have since become household words. G. M. Trevelyan, E. M. Forster, and Ivor Brown, the last fresh from Oxford, were teaching. Bernard Pitt, ill at ease as a civilian in wartime, carried on teaching for a year; and when on leave later on, made College history by bringing his wife to sit and talk among the men in the common-room. On the domestic side Mrs Simmons, the caretaker's wife, continued in her own job as cook and kept her husband's work going also, while he was a prisoner of war in Holland.*

But the College lost some of her finest, most promising men. One thinks of Wetenhall, handsome, witty, learned and gay, and of Robert Bailey, a fine teacher, earnest and lovable, who enlisted on the outbreak of war, and died in Palestine. Both seemed destined for positions of leadership. The losses suffered by the College cannot be measured . . . but they were heavy and grievous.

And so the College carried on through the war years, and the end found the old traditions intact, although serious problems of finance and reorganization remained to be tackled.

Among the 'middle young' aged men whose efforts had helped to keep things going were Sweetman, J. Flynn and Isaake, while the College ladies, as yet unorganized, but led by Mrs Lionel Jacob, 'did their bit' in the provision of comforts for the troops and in services generally. . . . The old guard, Lucas, Jacob, Lupton, Duchesne and others, survived to hand on to the new men a going concern, depleted in strength, but still vital. Men returning from overseas settled down in the College again with a minimum of fuss. As one of them said, 'You return after four years, and people just come in and say "hello, So-and-So".' A minor feature of change after the war was the absence

* Mrs Simmons, widowed after the First World War, was an indefatigable worker in the 1939 W.M.C. Ladies' War Work Party.

from the common-room of the foreign element, quite notable in the old days. . . .*

I do not remember the details of Founders' Days, College Sports and Furnivall Treats. Some events certainly took place, modified by wartime conditions. . . . Corporal Christie, a College student, won the V.C., an event that made a considerable impact on the College. . . . There were societies that grew up during the war and faded out of existence at its close, as, for instance, the Furnivall Literary Society. The Bernard Pitt Reading Circle was a war-time creation that survived for half a century. The Oswald Modern Languages Club and the Debating Society, always a vigorous institution, flourished throughout the war.

* It returned later, in force.

by A. J. W. Walker,

SIR CHARLES LUCAS, K.C.B., K.C.M.G.
Vice-Principal 1897–1903, Principal 1912–22

ARTHUR S. LUPTON
Vice-Principal 1911-21

III

SOME IMPORTANT PEOPLE AND A HERO IN THE COLLEGE

THE College has been fortunate in attracting men of great qualities to its service. Their impact has been strong and lasting. No description of the place in any given period can be complete without some account of the men who so powerfully influenced its policies, and were responsible for guiding its destinies.

The Principal in 1914 was Sir Charles Lucas; tall and bearded, with a slight stoop, gentle and courteous, with a quiet unexpected dry humour, a bachelor, he had that indefinable quality often associated with unassuming people, that sets them a little apart from other men, and wins a deference without either expecting or demanding it. Chaucer's 'very parfaite gentil knighte' always seemed to me a perfect description of Sir Charles Lucas.

Lionel Jacob, a former Vice-Principal and a member of the Executive Committee, was a similar type, gentle and scholarly, with a mild sense of humour; but in contrast to Lucas he was short and stocky, and slightly fussy in manner. He had much of Lucas's wisdom, but lacked his unselfconscious natural aristocratic dignity. Incidentally, it was Lionel Jacob who introduced his nephew Ellis Franklin to the College in 1919.

In striking contrast to Lucas and Jacob was the Vice-Principal, Arthur Lupton. Fair, ruddy, clean shaven, bluff and cheerful – his stock mode of address to an audience at College

SOME IMPORTANT PEOPLE AND A HERO

meetings and functions was 'Friends All' – He was friendly and informal; easy to get on with, and enjoyed his popularity. An active supporter of the sports clubs he was to be seen most weekends at the playing fields, and was what in modern slang would be termed 'hearty'.

Leonard Pocock, Chairman of the Marks Fellowship and of the Old Students' Club, was a familiar figure in the commonroom. A solicitor by profession, he had been both student and teacher at the College, and after the war held the office of Bursar, till failing health obliged him to retire. He was succeeded by Ellis Franklin.

Of Marks – whose name is perpetuated in the Marks Fellowship, that benevolent society of the College – Wetenhall and Bailey, Bernard Pitt and Bromhall, I have no personal memory, but they were giants in their day, and well loved in the College. Their names appear later in this book.

Duchesne, for many years the Superintendent, a strong personality, with an energetic, breezy manner, was a considerable force in the College. Its officers leaned heavily on him and he rendered them great service throughout the war. He was typical of his generation, devoted, idealistic, but lacking the vision to see with the eyes of the new age.

In 1916 a student, L/Cpl Christie, brought honour and glory to the College by winning the V.C.

Christie was a railway clerk at Euston Station. He joined the college in 1911 and attended classes in French, algebra, elementary science, geometry, chemistry, electricity and shorthand. Of Scottish descent he was a fine sportsman, and played (football?) for a Holloway team, the whole of which volunteered for service when the war broke out, Christie himself joining up in September 1914.

The citation for his decoration in the *London Gazette*, February 1918, describes the award as being for 'most conspicuous bravery. When, after a position had been captured, the enemy immediately made counter bombing attacks up communication trenches, Lance Corporal Christie, realizing the position, took a supply of bombs over the top, proceeding alone about fifty yards in the open along the communication trench, and bombed the enemy. He continued to do this alone in spite of heavy

SOME IMPORTANT PEOPLE AND A HERO

opposition until a block had been established. Returning towards our lines he heard voices behind him; he at once turned back and bombed another party moving up the trench, entirely breaking up a further bombing attack. By his prompt action ... he undoubtedly cleared a difficult position at a most critical time and saved many lives. Throughout he was subjected to heavy machine-gun fire, and shellfire. He showed the greatest coolness and a total disregard for his own safety.'

Christie was wounded both before and after the events recorded above. His return home to receive his decoration was delayed because, as the *Journal* remarks, he 'could not be spared from the Palestine front, where he was again wounded in March, in the knee and wrist, and was sent to hospital. . . . His portrait has been framed and hung up in the College . . .'

Two letters from Christie will be found among the letters from 'countries other than France', that are collected together in this volume. But the few lines quoted below seem to belong in this place:
From L/Cpl Christie V.C., to a friend in the College.

'*Egypt* . . . Am still in this land of eternal sunshine, hoping to leave it any day now. Am awaiting a boat which may mean a few days or as many weeks . . .'

Below this fragment, which appears in the *Journal*, printed in block letters is the triumphant announcement:

CHRISTIE IS BACK WITH US. HOORAY!

On December 14th, 1918, a great reception was given to Christie at what was called 'The Ladies' Concert of W.M.C. Musical Society', when Christie was presented with 'a clock and some books', somewhat pompously described in the *Journal* as 'a gift from his fellow members and friends in the College in recognition of the brave and valorous deed performed by him for which he was awarded the Victoria Cross'. The ladies presented the hero with a fountain-pen.

Sir Charles Lucas was in the cahir on this auspicious occasion, and read out a letter from Sir Frederick Maurice regretting his

SOME IMPORTANT PEOPLE AND A HERO

inability to be present 'owing to his absence in France'. After which 'was sung the hymn "O God, our help in ages past".'

Following upon the hymn, Sir Charles Lucas seems to have been unable to resist the temptation to give one of his long – and, it must be realized – popular dissertations, full of highminded and wise reflections on the war.

After this Tom Barnard, elocution teacher, recited Kipling's 'Recessional'. 'Christie stood to attention and saluted, and was heartily cheered.'

After another speech, brief but laudatory, from Sir Charles, and a short, modest reply from Christie, who remarked that he would 'always strive to be worthy of the great honour the College had done him', three cheers were called for the hero, and 'three more for Mrs Christie, who was present'. The concert was then allowed to proceed.

IV

WORK PARTIES AND MARKS FELLOWSHIP

THE formation of ladies' work parties in the two world wars opens up a whole chapter of College history. The first point of interest that strikes one, looking back, is the immediate and spontaneous reaction of the College ladies in both periods, turning the instinctive urge to help to practical and prompt account. On each occasion the wife of a Vice-Principal – in the case of the First World War an ex-Vice-Principal – was in the fortunate position of being able to channel the upsurge of warm-hearted goodwill in a useful direction.

The opportunities for service open to the work party of the Second World War were wider, and full advantage was taken of this fact. It was in all its aspects more essentially a College affair, based on the College and working in close association with its students and staff.

Throughout the First World War, Mrs Lionel Jacob's ladies met every month at her home – often they brought their children with them – for work and tea and a pleasantly sociable afternoon; greatly to the benefit of the men in the services.

The position is neatly summed up in a note in the *Journal* in July 1917. 'Mrs Lionel Jacob's work parties,' it says, 'continue to contribute gifts of knitted and other articles [usually food] for the comfort of our soldiers and sailors. Socks are especially wanted [so they were in 1939 and onwards!] and will be still more in demand as the year wears on. The Comforts Fund as well as the Marks Fellowship general funds will welcome contributions from donors old and new. . . . The Comforts Fund acknowledges the receipt of £14 14s. 11d., the proceeds of the Gilbert and Sullivan Concert given by the Musical Society.'

The Marks Fellowship and the Old Students' Club felt the important duty of keeping in touch with College men in the Forces was essentially their mission. The priorities in the Second World War were the same, only the organization for giving them effect was different. The French have the right phrase for it – 'Plus ça change, plus c'est la même chose.'

Almost from the outbreak of the war the *Journal* is peppered with little notes referring to the Comforts Fund. . . . Thus at Christmas time 1915, readers are reminded that 'there is no fund or object at the College at the present time so worthy of support as the Comforts Fund'. The note continues in the somewhat preaching manner of the day: 'We owe a great debt of gratitude to the 200 of our members who are beyond the seas serving in the forces, and it is intended to send each one a Christmas parcel, the principal item in which will be a pair of woollen socks costing about 3s. 3d. . . . the other contents [which included a Christmas pudding!] will bring the cost of each parcel up to about 6s., so that £60 will be required. Subscriptions earmarked 'Comforts Fund' will be gladly received by the Treasurer of the Marks Fellowship . . .'

With the war still dragging on into the spring of 1918, the Comforts Fund continues to be a matter of concern in the College, and a note in the May issue of the *Journal* reports that 'the College had its first Tombola. . . . The Tombola resulted in a profit of over £30 for the Marks Fellowship Comforts Fund.'

Marks Fellowship and Old Students' Club, 1915
'. . . For some months past the members of the committee have been engaged in writing letters to those College soldiers of whom nothing had been heard for some time. In all about two hundred letters have been written, asking the men to reply giving their correct addresses, so that the *Journal* might be forwarded to them, and assuring them of the earnest desire of the College to keep in touch with them, and to welcome them back when the war is over. It is gratifying to add that a great

WORK PARTIES AND MARKS FELLOWSHIP

number of very interesting replies have been received – and are still arriving – from all fronts, from France, Mesopotamia, Salonica, Egypt, the Sinai desert; some written in German dug-outs in France, others from our trenches, some from Baghdad and beyond, and some from hospitals, convalescent homes, and training camps in England. As might be expected of College men, many of the letters told of promotion, both in commissioned and non-commissioned rank, and all of them breathed the writers' love for the College and its associations, their appreciation of the interest taken in them by the College, and, in a number of cases, their determination to take a larger part in the work of the College on returning to civil life.'

In May 1915 the editor of the *Journal* observes in a note that he 'would be much obliged if those readers who are serving with the forces would kindly acknowledge receipt of this month's *Journal* when it reaches them, so that he may know whether the copies posted go astray or duly arrive at their intended destination'.

The *Journal* seems to have come out monthly, unhindered by the horrid spectre of paper rationing, that made such frequent publication impossible in the Second World War.

V

ON THE WAR—STUDENT TEACHER MEETINGS

STUDENT teacher meetings on the war were held regularly every month, usually under the chairmanship of Sir Charles Lucas, with a guest speaker to give an address or open a discussion.

At the first of these, held in May 1915, G. M. Trevelyan was the guest speaker. But he had to do some listening before he was allowed to speak!

The proceedings opened with some introductory remarks by Sir Charles Lucas, who explained that this was the first of a series of monthly meetings which they hoped would be addressed by College men who had themselves been at the front. . . . 'In this war,' he said, 'democracy was on its trial, England was fighting to secure the right to live to little nations, and if the victory was to be gained everyone must faithfully do his part . . .' There followed sundry wise admonitions and comments, and in conclusion Sir Charles said that he 'wished to emphasize that we were out to see that these small peoples have their life and their say in the world. They are all doing their part and it is for us to stand firm. The whole world is looking at England and remembering our past, and it is for us to do so too.'

After Lucas had spoken, Bob Hagerty, a deservedly popular College character, had his say, and finally Starling reported on the work of the College Volunteer Reserves – a report that was something of a damp squib.

STUDENT TEACHER MEETINGS

'The Corps had been rather a disappointment in numbers,' he said, 'of some eighty men who had promised to join, only about thirty had turned up. They had learnt all they could in the confined space of the gymnasium, and had been inspected by Major Wood of the Hampstead Volunteer Reserve . . . with which Corps they would probably affiliate . . .'

Now at last the guest of the evening was allowed to make his speech. Its subject was Serbia (now Yugoslavia) and part of the speech is worth reproducing for the picture it gives of that country in 1915.* 'The example of this little country,' the speaker said, 'is by far the greatest that the war has yet produced. The reason why Serbians are more heroic and patriotic when it comes to fighting for their country is because they are more entirely single-minded than any other country in Europe, for they have nothing to think about except their country. There are no politics and no class distinctions in Serbia. There is only one class, the class of the peasant proprietors . . . they have not yet got to the industrial stage or to the class questions which arise out of it . . . there is no feudal class or landlords, the Turks killed them all off before they went away.

'Serbia is a true democracy socially and economically. . . . The great disadvantage of this condition arises from the fact that there is no class with leadership traditions of any sort. . . . The best of their educated class goes into the army . . . the mingled discipline and comradeship of the Serbian army is a very fine thing to see . . .'

The speaker continued a fascinating dissertation describing the horrors of the Austro-Hungarian invasion of Serbia, and the atrocities committed on the civilian population by the invaders, because 'it puts an end to the idea that the Balkan peoples are on a lower level than the other races. . . . Further he did not think that the Serbians had taken reprisals. Sixty thousand Austrian prisoners had been taken; he had talked to many of them and had not heard one complain of his treatment by his captors . . . wounded were treated in the hospitals on an absolute equality with Serbians.'

At the conclusion of what proved to be an informative and fascinating account of the history and conduct of the Balkan

* Not all modern historians would endorse Trevelyan's views on Serbia in the First World War.

part of the war, there were yet more speeches, and the meeting closed on a gentle note of anti-climax, with the pious hope expressed by Sir Charles Lucas that 'these monthly meetings would help us to bear the war in mind and to remember that we have our part to play in this great crisis'.

It is perhaps not generally known in the college that in 1916 the King of Italy presented a silver medal to G. M. Trevelyan for 'gallantry under heavy shellfire in removing patients while in charge of a British ambulance in Italy'. Almost throughout the war Trevelyan served in the Italian Red Cross, in Italy.

Mr Fraser, a College teacher, home on leave from the front in France – returned thanks to Trevelyan for his address. In the course of his speech these remarks occur. 'The first time I was under fire,' he said, 'I lay down in a ditch, the next man in a heap of cow dung. There was no trouble in teaching men to take cover, they did it by instinct . . .' 'When their turn came to go to the trenches,' he relates, 'they set out in no very cheerful frame of mind . . . Very heavily laden they went off in single file to the trenches, perhaps a mile away, through fields knee deep in mud, and crept along a road deep in mud, quiet as cats, for the Germans had a machine-gun trained on it. . . . Ultimately you dived into your trench; sometimes it was very wet and you could only talk to the next man when he came up out of the mud to breathe. . . .' He had 'seen men break down under the strain of the trenches and sob like children, but when their time came to go in again they were quite ready and cheerful. The British Tommy has no end of guts.' Their days were not always so trying. Sometimes they were billeted at a farm, when they would 'look round for some fowls, and in the evening have a concert to which they would invite a neighbouring battalion. . . . Sir Charles had spoken of democracy. He, Fraser, did not understand democracy. It always seemed to him a question whether democracy would voluntarily submit to discipline. When a man enters the army he has to do as he is d— well told. He often wondered whether democracy would do it.'

Mr Fraser's remarks are so apt to the problems of the 1960's that it seemed worth while including them here.

At the meeting 'On the War' in July 1915, Sir Charles Lucas was the speaker. The speech, as a whole, is of no particular interest today, but one or two isolated sentences are worth quoting. He observes that 'The colour has gone out of the landscape, the heavy greens succeeding the lighter shades of the early season . . . the war has become monotonous, dragging out with more shadow than light. . . . All our wars have been long and wearying, and we have pulled through in the end. . . . Two things, and only two, will do it, patience and unity. Patience is hard for a democracy to learn. . . . Let us all speak with one voice . . . we must all fight this out to the end, suffering no compromise of any sort or kind. There cannot be a compromise about right or wrong; there cannot be a compromise about freedom. You will have men here and there saying "stop the war", but *the pacificists are the makers of war in time to come* . . .'

A somewhat surprising address in the monthly series of talks 'On the War' at the Old Students' Club Meetings was given by Mr Edmund Maurice. He called it 'Hints from the War'. Although of the family of the Founder, he was assuredly no 'chip off the old block', for Mr Maurice was a pacifist and read a most provocative paper.

Hard upon this somewhat disconcerting incident came the pleasant news that Lieutenant-Colonel F. B. Maurice, a grandson of Frederick Denison, and destined between the wars to become Principal of the College, had been 'mentioned in dispatches' from the front. He was to win far greater honour, and, almost at the height of a meteoric rise in his profession, was to sacrifice the military career that was so dear to him in the cause of patriotism and honour, and what he deemed to be his duty. The story does not belong to these pages, but it is a record of quiet moral heroism.

The New Army

On Monday, November 30th, 1915, a well-attended students' and teachers' meeting was held in the common-room, under the chairmanship of the Principal, to hear Captain Wetenhall on 'The New Army'.

In his opening remarks Sir Charles Lucas said: 'I am sorry and glad that A. H. Perry* has gone to serve his country and take charge of the music for the R.N.R. I apologize for myself,

* Father of the once well-known comedian, the late Laddie Cliff – died after the Second World War. For many years an old student of the College.

who have hardly fired a gun and once drilled for an hour. In my mind as I speak, and in the minds of all right-minded men in my place, comes the question: Why do you urge people to do what you are not doing yourself? I am now advancing in years; my eyesight is not good; if I enlisted I should have difficulty in hitting even the big drum. A man like me ought not to speak to others about going to the war, unless he is absolutely, from the bottom of his heart, convinced it is the right thing to do. I am convinced. Why? First, we did all we could to avoid war. Every statesman ought to do all he can to prevent this great scourge of war, bringing untold miseries to families and nations, making innumerable widows and orphans, and leaving a legacy of bitterness which it takes generations to forget.

'Sir Edward Grey did all a man could do to prevent this great scourge. Secondly, we were bound by our word of honour – by that "scrap of paper" of which we have heard so much and shall hear more – bound to defend the independence of Belgium. We could not have gone back on our word without losing our place, deservedly, among the nations. Some of you may think we should never give such a bond again. I do not agree. I hold that nations, like men, cannot say, "Am I my brother's keeper?" Nations cannot stand outside their duties, and I hope England, bound as she is, will stand by her bond and protect the smaller nations that are near her shores. Thirdly, it is as clear to me as daylight that Germany wished to reduce France to a state of vassalage. If there were no Belgium in the case, I say that England would have been bound to stand up and see that France preserved her national independence and her national life. Fourthly, it is clear that Germany evidently aimed at us ourselves. If you read Bernhardi's book, *Germany and the Next War* you will find it all planned out there. They were prepared to break France first, then turn on Russia, and finally in a few years to strike their great enemy, England.'

Private Dell, H.A.C.,* who also had a hearty greeting, narrated his feelings in regard to enlisting, how he felt, like a racehorse, that he 'ought to be there'. Like Hepburn and others, he had become a special constable, but that didn't seem enough. One night while on police duty a hefty coal-heaver, slightly 'on the tiddley', came up to him, gave a salute, pulled a paper out

* Honourable Artillery Company – a territorial unit.

of his pocket, and said, 'That's what I've done – been and joined the army, and I'm off tomorrow to shoot them —— Germans what butchered the Belgians.' It seemed to Dell that the coaley was inspired with the right idea, determined to do his little bit, and so why shouldn't he? And he joined. While with the H.A.C. he met with a case of a miner who had a wife and child and who wanted to join, but was doubtful about how the wife would take it, until one night she solved the problem by saying to him, 'Tomorrow morning you go and join the army.' On which he went straight away and did it. 'Training had a wonderful effect on men, rendering them more fit, inspiring them with the right sort of feeling, and it had a solidifying effect on the whole regiment. He would like to have Wetenhall* as a leader: he felt he could follow such a man anywhere.' (Cheers.)

... Mr Lionel Jacob (an ex-Vice-Principal) said that 'no price was too high to pay for English order and liberty. ... The military authorities said, 'Come and help us, or we cannot be sure of saving you.' They asked for all the help they could get, and who would deny it at a time like this?'

... Sir Charles Lucas, in voicing thanks to Captain Wetenhall and those who had spoken after him, said 'he remembered reading in *The Life of Sir Frederick Maurice* that the next war would not be fought on the sacred soil of England. But we were fighting as much for our liberty on the soil of Belgium and France as if the struggle were going on here on the soil of England – for our liberty, our national strength, and our national existence. There could be no cause more inspiring for Englishmen and for College men.'

Captain Wetenhall (of the 6th Leicesters) nominally the main speaker at this meeting on The New Army, is briefly reported, after the speeches just quoted, in a single paragraph in the *Journal*. He appears to have made a stirring recruiting speech, in which he referred to himself as the 'British born descendent of a Flemish refugee, with a few drops of Belgian blood in me'. He described the preposterously unready state of things at Aldershot when war broke out; his own experiences training the Leicestershire regiment; the bravery of our troops at the front, and more in the same strain, concluding with an

---

* Wetenhall; teacher, chairman of the Studies Committee – one of the bright young men of the College.

impassioned appeal for every fit man to join the fighting services.

It is interesting to observe that the next item in the *Journal*, after all this inspired patriotism, is headed 'Shakespeare Readings'. Something more than a sense of balance had been preserved in the College!

VI

FOUNDERS' NIGHTS AND OTHER COLLEGE OCCASIONS

Founders' Day, 1914

WAR with Germany was declared by Great Britain on August 4th, 1914. A wave of emotional patriotism broke over the country. Men in their thousands rushed to enlist in the fighting services. But a slogan of the times, in strange contrast to this vigorous militancy, was the government's admonition to carry on with 'Business as Usual'.

Within the College much of its life flowed on unchanged. Its functions took place at their appointed times, though with depleted numbers.

In October 1914 Founders' Night was celebrated with an extra flourish, since it fell in the Jubilee year of the founding of the College.

The opening paragraph of the *Journal*'s account of the proceedings, reproduced below, is revealing.

'Sixty years had passed when on Saturday, October 31st, we met to celebrate the foundation of the College – sixty years of all kinds of success, little and great; years of adversity and of prosperity; years of gladness and of sorrow. Much like a man's life has been the life of the College. Conceived in a time of trouble out of high resolve, sacrifice and love of man for fellow man; fostered by earnest purpose and enthusiastic zeal. . . . By sacrificing anew and still by love, it has maintained its purpose and has reached its present high estate. . . . 'The College, on this its sixtieth anniversary, finds itself as a man of British birth and equal age finds himself, under the stress and strain, the uncertain and unmeasured impulse of the world's greatest war. As do such a man's sons, so do members of the College leave it, to fight for their country and their honour. . . .'

In his speech Sir Charles Lucas, the Principal, reminded his audience that the College was founded in the year of the outbreak of the Crimean War, and moved from Great Ormond Street to its present premises in the year of the Boer War. 'It celebrates its Jubilee in a clash of arms far greater, far nobler, far nearer our own homes than the Crimean War . . . we all know the evils of war. . . . In 1814 England was coming to the end of her great war against the despotism of Napoleon. . . . In 1914 we are standing, thank God, against military despotism. . . .' (Cheers.)

It was a long speech, invoking the dead voices of the Founders on the subjects of discipline, and the inspiration of the call of duty in a great cause. It was a fine speech, typical of the man, and of the moment.

Another interesting feature of this 1914 Founders' Night lies in some of the names associated with it, that link the college so closely with its Founders.

The Reverend Llewelyn Davies and Professor Dicey sent messages of regret at being unable to be present. Among the guests were Miss May Hughes (sister of Tom Hughes, the author of *Tom Brown's School Days*, one of the Founders of the College) and the Misses Lowes Dickenson with their married sister, and Mrs Tansley. There were a host of others, but these stand out for their early association with the great men of the College.

Founders' Nights continued to be celebrated until 1917, in contrast to the shape of things in 1939, when all major functions at the College immediately ceased.

Founders' Night and College Art, 1915

Founders' Night, October 1915 was commemorated by a gathering in the common-room and coffee-room, the Maurice

Hall having been requisitioned as the recruiting station for the district.

Sir Charles Lucas gave the address, and various exhibitions had been arranged in the College by the students, including the art classes. The report of the proceedings in the *Journal* gives in full Lucas's speech which has no particular interest today and discusses the 'very creditable exhibition' arranged by the Art Class and Sketching Club. There were paintings in water-colour and oils, drawings and portraits; two of the artists received praise for 'their very good oil-paintings of trees and landscapes'. Other items singled out for particular commendation included 'a clever copy in oils of one of Solomon's pictures . . . a good water-colour copy of Calnan's landscapes and figures', and by the principal art teacher 'many military pictures'. From which account it may be surmised that even by the standards of that time the art classes could hardly be described as 'modern' in aim or achievement.

Founders' Night, 1916

'Founders' Day,' reports the *Journal*, 'was marked by one of our Principal's splendid addresses, and by a speech, reminiscent in character, by Major General Maurice. 'Sweet are the uses of Adversity,' quoted the Principal, 'especially in this respect; that in these times long speeches are more abhorred than ever, even by those who listen – much more by those who try to make them.' He then proceeded, very successfully, to make one. His theme was 'Lest we forget', and the address falls somewhere between a sermon and a discursive talk. Maurice followed with some lively personal recollections of the Founders, most of whom he had met at some time or other. 'I well remember,' he relates, 'being taken as a very small boy to the old building in Great Ormond Street, and being set on by Tom Hughes to fight the office boy. . . . I remember he had been under Tom Hughes' instruction longer than I had.' Maurice also told how he had, at his grandfather's request, been left with him (Frederick Denison Maurice) in his study while he wrote a sermon for Christmas Day, on childhood. 'I was placed on the hearth-rug with a toy or two, and he, at his desk, was writing the sermon. As he wrote he threw the leaves, one after the other, on the floor. I soon discovered that the fallen sheets of white paper were more

FOUNDERS' NIGHTS AND OTHER OCCASIONS

attractive than my toys, and one by one they made a glorious blaze on the fire . . .' He continues in a more serious vein speaking of the outstanding qualities of the Founders, which he names as 'nobleness of aim, honesty of purpose, love of truth, and perhaps most of all, love of their fellow men'.

Social Gatherings

'Every Saturday night during the vacation,' says a note in the *Journal* of July 1915, 'social gatherings will be held at the College from 8.30 till 10.30. All College students and their lady friends are invited. Specially welcome are the relations and friends of men serving in H.M. Forces who may be glad of the opportunity to keep in touch with the College. . . . Music is provided (by members of the College), there will be songs and recitations by the people present.' The first of these gatherings took place in August and met with considerable success. About forty were present, including a number of men on leave from the Middle East and other parts of the world. Yarns were exchanged, one man humorously explaining that his visits to hospital were due to misadventures with a motor cycle and not to shrapnel. 'Several of the Hampstead Brigade [of the Volunteer Training Corps?] attended. Mr and Mrs Lionel Jacob came in to wish us all success.'

During the Second World War a feature was made of Friday nights, when men foregathered in the superintendent's room for coffee and beer and talk. Ladies were not invited to these weekly socials, but their contact with the College was well maintained through work-party meetings and functions and was very much alive.

The urge to keep in touch was manifest in both world wars, and seems a peculiarly pleasing expression of the close ties that exist between the College and her sons, and that had come to mean so much to men in those harsh times, even in the farthest corners of the earth.

By 1918 aspects of College life, subdued by the war, were stirring to renewed activity.

The following note on *The Sketching Club* is typical of this phase.

As late as October 1918, at the opening meeting of the

FOUNDERS' NIGHTS AND OTHER OCCASIONS

Common-Room Committee, the troubles of the Sketching Club are thought worth including in its report. '"Dora" (Defence of the Realm Act, 1914)* and the jumpiness of the public's nerves over the matter of German spies have made it advisable for the Sketch Club to suspend their out-of-door activities. Driven back on their own resources they have met at the College throughout the year with such good results that they have the material ready for an art exhibition, and have kept the machinery in order for a grand offensive when conditions permit of a resumption of their outings.'

In November 1918 the *Journal* gives an account of a lecture given by Sir Frederick Maurice in the Maurice Hall on the Campaign of 1918 in the West, 'How our Victories were Won', the Chair being taken by Sir Charles Lucas. Thus there sat in the hall together a present and a future Principal of the College. It was also a foretaste of the time to come that, as the *Journal* reported, 'Lady Maurice and her family' were in the audience. 'It is very delightful,' the Chairman pointed out, 'that General Maurice has chosen what would be Founders' Day to give us a lecture.' The lecturer responded in his opening remarks, 'I feel it a very real honour that it should have fallen to me this evening to reopen the Maurice Hall. Somehow it really does seem to bring peace in sight. When I suggested to Pocock that instead of opening a debate for the Old Students' Club, I should come and tell you something about the war, I had no idea that I should be honoured by such an audience or should have the very great distinction of, in a humble way, replacing the celebration of Founders' Day in this Hall.'

The simple unaffected modesty of these opening observations by Maurice are so characteristic of the man that they seem worth quoting for the true picture that they give of a Principal of the College who exemplified in his person the finest tradition of the place.

A New Year's Greeting
      (Written for the *Journal* in January 1917 by
            Sir Charles Lucas)

---

* The final death of 'Dora' was not achieved for a number of years after peace had been signed.

FOUNDERS' NIGHTS AND OTHER OCCASIONS

Fellow Members of the Working Men's College:

'The year which has just closed has been memorable in the history of the College. The last of our Founders has passed away (Llewelyn Davies) and leading men in the ranks of present-day teachers and students have given their lives that we may live.

'We enter on the New Year with reduced numbers and straitened resources, but with pride and thankfulness that our brethren have placed before our eyes such noble examples of service and sacrifice – the watchwords of the College – and that at home and abroad the College spirit burns with greater intensity than ever.

'To our men at the front we send a message of heartfelt gratitude for upholding our good name, illustrating our principles, and linking our college with faithfulness unto death.

'To all on this side or beyond the seas we send assurance that in the coming year we will strive to quit us like men, and be strong to abjure sluggishness, and waste; to endure hardships, to wait patiently, and to work for the good time which will surely come, when the right shall prevail and the peoples of the world, small and great alike, shall have abiding peace.

'On behalf of the College,
C. P. Lucas.'

This is included as a period piece. It may be a cause for regret that modern inhibitions would make an exhortation in such terms almost ludicrous today. The 'simple faith' has been destroyed by events, many past our power to control; there is disillusionment, and an adolescent shrinking from expressing deeper feelings explicitly, in elegant or emotional language.

In December 1916 Sir Charles Lucas composed a New Year greeting in verse, that he had printed on postcards with a view of the College 'and sent to all members of the forces who had notified their whereabouts!'

> Brothers who stand for your motherland
> Be it friend, be it foe you are meeting;
> Christmas goodwill be with you still
> And a College New Year greeting.

In 1943 the greeting on the Christmas card sent to the men in the Forces was also a home manufactured verse. So the wheel goes round full circle.

War weariness was combined with optimism in 1943, and the feeling is expressed in the lines written for the Christmas card of that year.

> CHRISTMAS 1943
> Five Christmastides of war,
> Five years rolled by
> Heavy with poignant memory.
> Ring out old year,
> You shall unsorrowed die.
> Ring in new year
> With teeming hope raised high,
> That at your close
> War clouds that vex'd the old
> Shall as a passing tale be told,
> And peace on earth
> Goodwill to men
> To living truth
> Shall be translated then.

These hopeful lines went out a year too soon, but by the end of 1943 the parting of the darkest clouds was in sight.

VII

JOTTINGS FROM THE JOURNAL

'WE owe it to the war,' the *Journal* comments in 1915, 'that there will be no College Sports this year, nor visits to Oxford or Cambridge, nor Cricket Club.' The College of course at that time had no playing field of its own, but the brief announcement cancelling all games for the duration of the war pinpoints an interesting contrast in restrictions at the College between the First and Second World Wars. While in 1914–18 a remarkable degree of normal College life, both social and academic, was able to survive, and sports activities lapsed completely, in 1939 to 1945, thanks in part to the College being the owner of its playing field, and in part to the Pavilion being in occupation by a friendly group of Civil Defence Workers, cricket, football, bowls, and even tennis, continued in a limited degree throughout the war, though academic and social life in the College suffered considerably, especially in the worst periods of the air attack on London.

Another note in the *Journal* in 1915 requests 'readers having copies of Charlin's *French Text Book*, Parts 1, 2 or 3, to kindly forward same to the College if they can spare them, for the use of students in the coming year. Copies of this excellent text book cannot now be obtained. . . .' The significance of this paragraph is the pointer it gives to the existence in 1915 of flourishing French classes in the college. Two inconsequential pieces of information follow on the announcement of the cancellation of all College sports activities. 'It has been decided,' the *Journal* states, 'not to print the Calendar.' And last, but perhaps not least, 'Mr Harold Scott has sent 10s. 6d. to the fund which is being raised for the College section of Volunteers.'

In 1916 death had struck heavily at the College. Llewelyn Davies, the last surviving member of the Founders, died full of years, but two College men, Wetenhall and Bromhall, both killed in action, were young and full of promise of future achievement. The College could ill afford to lose such men. Extracts from the Obituary Notices in the *Journal* are given below:

July 1916. 'A FATHER OF THE COLLEGE.'
'On the 18th May Mr Llewelyn Davies died. Those of us who were present at the funeral, simple, restful, and harmonious, in Hampstead Church and churchyard, felt that a great link with the past had been severed, but that more than one rich memory and noble example had been added to our Roll of Honour. Born in 1826, he was in his 91st year when he died. I want to say a word of him as a man and as a Founder.

'He was essentially a strong man.... A son of Cambridge and a Fellow of Trinity, as were also three of his sons, he was a scholar of high repute and a fine Alpine climber.... If he had never done or written anything else, his name would be handed down as the joint author of one of the best and most successful translations that has ever been made.... Davies and Vaughan's Translation of Plato's *Republic.*

'Davies was one of the great Cambridge school of theologians, alike virile and reverent, who brought scholarship and scholarly criticism to bear upon theological questions. But he was much more, he was a worker and a teacher among men. His life work was that of a clergyman of the Church of England, and his experience ranged from the East End of London and Christchurch, Marylebone, to Kirkby Lonsdale in the remote valleys of Westmorland. Liberal alike in religion and politics, he was heart and soul a follower of Frederick Denison Maurice. Like Maurice, he never received the preferment which was his due. But no one ever lived who angled less for the favours of fortune than Llewelyn Davies. He was an educational reformer, a lifelong supporter of a wider field for women, being for a time Principal of Queen's College, Harley Street, and for many years Chairman of the Governing body of the Working Women's College in Fitzroy Street.'

WILLIAM THORNTON WETENHALL, *killed in action in Palestine, July 1916.*

'The heaviest blow yet struck at the College by the War has taken from us Captain W. T. Wetenhall, of the 6th Leicester Regiment, who was killed in action on Sunday, July 16th, 1916. The news came upon the College with numbing effect, just as the Studies Committee, of which he was Chairman before the war, was about to meet. He stood, as Mr Jacob has pointed out, third man in the College, coming next to the Vice-Principal. As Chairman of the Studies Committee, member of the Council and Executive Committee, Director of Studies in the Modern Languages Section; organizer of classes, class-work, and examinations; teacher of the Advanced German class, President of the Oswald Modern Languages Club, examiner and helper in many different ways, Wetenhall was one of the most valuable and capable men in the College.'

MAJOR JOHN BROMHALL, *killed in action in France.*

'Among the many students of the College who have given up their lives for their country . . . is Major John Bromhall, M.C., and Bar, the son of one of our oldest students, Mr John Bromhall.

'By profession, a jeweller, he at once volunteered when war broke out, but was rejected as medically unfit owing to varicose veins, so went into hospital to have the veins removed. As soon as he was fit again he obtained a commission in the Sherwood Foresters. He served in France.'

The citation for his decoration quotes 'his brave defence of the road from Cambrai to Bapaume during the German offensive (of March 1916) . . . it was due to him and his company of machine-gunners, among others, that the progress of the enemy along that road was checked . . .' He was wounded in that attack and sent home to hospital. He then learnt he was promoted to the rank of Major and had won the M.C. for the second time. . . . He went out to France again on July 29th and was killed by a fragment of shell on August 7th while inspecting his gun positions in a quiet section of the line.

JOTTINGS FROM THE JOURNAL

These jottings from the *Journal* in 1719 give a glimpse of the way College life was going on at this time.

There was a choir concert in May 'in the common- and coffee-rooms, the Vice-Principal was in the chair.' This was the only purely social event arranged in that summer.

Teachers' Meeting, 1917

'On June 1st a general meeting of the teachers was arranged by the Vice-Principal and the Chairman of the Studies Committee. The proceedings commenced with a supper . . . and after supper the business part of the meeting was held in the common-room. Unfortunately the Vice-Principal was prevented from attending at the last moment by a sudden attack of illness, so Mr Lionel Jacob took his place. . . . There were about thirty teachers present. The meeting and discussion were quite a success, and part of the time was spent in considering suggestions for development in certain directions when war shall have ceased to upset the College and its work.'

'On June 2nd the Shakespeare Society held their annual tea and concluding meeting of the session . . .'

'On June 28th the hon. secretaries and others interested in the various College societies were entertained to supper by the Vice-Principal, and after supper the dates of the proposed meetings were discussed and settled.

'The hostel plan again came up for discussion, Mr Hepburn the Chairman of the Marks Fellowship being "responsible for its exhumation".'

COLLEGE PHOTOGRAPHER

In a lighter vein is the account of the 'College Photographers'. 'Mr (Alexander) Hepburn,' runs the report, in July 1918, 'still pursues the taking of College war-time photographs with great zeal and varying success. Making a change from the method of one College photographer, who omitted to remove the cap for a flashlight exposure, Mr Hepburn removed the cap, but omitted to insert a plate in the camera. Thus, though the methods were dissimilar, the two operators arrived at an identical result.'*

* The old-fashioned camera had no automatic shutter. A contraption like a pill-box lid covered the lens. To take the picture, it had to be removed and replaced by hand.

VIII

OLD STUDENTS' SUPPERS AND TEAS 1914-18

THE Annual Old Students' Supper, traditionally held each December, took place without a break throughout the war, till 1917 when it was replaced by a tea. Some of the reports of these functions give a revealing glimpse of the College at that period, and of the way men's minds were turning.

The College Supper, December 19th, 1914
   'The thirty-eighth annual Supper of the Old Students' Club was held in the Maurice Hall on Saturday, December 19th, at 6.30 p.m., when 180 guests sat down to table, and scenes of great enthusiasm were witnessed. The Maurice Hall, having been used for the previous four months as the district recruiting station, was gaily decorated with military emblems, union jacks, and patriotic posters. A dozen willing helpers prepared the Hall and other rooms on the day. . . . When the tables had been laid with their snow-white cloths, with red strips down their centres, and with all the usual table decorations, the Hall looked really handsome, the portraits of the Founders on the platform being set off with a background of loyal colours. Many of the younger students and teachers were away, but there was a good attendance of those of maturer age, and many an old member met, and greeted at the assembly in the common room, friends he had not seen since the last supper. All the

events of the evening went with a swing. The Principal's speech was splendid, and the other speakers well maintained the usual high level. The shadow of the war did not cloud the proceedings, church-wardens* helped to do so. An excellent spirit prevailed, no one was downhearted,† the punch went down well; we thought of those who could not be with us, and the Furnivall Children's Treat collection raised the handsome sum of £8 2s. Mr Lionel Jacob brought with him as his guest, Professor Hamelius of the University of Liège, who had been through the siege of that place, had escaped to England, and was doing his work here.'

Pocock, proposing the toast of the College and its Principal, said, 'The Rev. Llewelyn Davies, the only surviving Founder of the College sends us his best wishes. . . . This year on Founders' Night, the College completed its 60th year.' 'The war,' he said, 'has reduced our membership, student entries were 1,281 for this term last year; this year they are 773, a drop of 508. As a rule, about half of the entries are old or regular students, and about half are new men each October term. The Marks Fellowship, an association of College men founded for College men in honour of the late President of this Club, Robert Marks, has made it its business to inquire into the reasons for the fall in numbers, in order that assistance might be given where wanted. . . . The result of its labours is satisfactory. It has been found that 140 students and twenty teachers are serving with the forces. The Executive Committee wisely decided to keep on the College roll the names of those who are serving their country. When we add the 140 soldier students to the number of old students who have rejoined, we find there has only been a fall in numbers of a dozen amongst the old students, a quarter of whom have enlisted. The drop in numbers is almost entirely due to the abstention from joining (the College) of those who would have been quite new students. This abstention is probably due largely to recruiting, short time, or extra work.'

Sir Charles Lucas, proposing the toast of 'College men with the Forces' and coupling with it the names of Lieutenant Bailey and Private Dell (Cheers), said: 'We all know Robert Bailey's

* A long stemmed claypipe it was a tradition to smoke at these suppers.

† Reference to a popular saying of the day, 'Are we downhearted?' to which the reply was a resounding 'no'.

energy and unselfishness and his devotion to the College. In Robert Bailey we are giving much to the war. . . . (Robert Bailey, later killed in action in France, was one of the bright, promising young teachers, destined for high office in the College had he survived the war.)

Lieut. Bailey, in reply, said he regretted that Wetenhall* was not there to 'pour out his eloquence on behalf of those who had been toasted', and he also wished there were present some of those men serving with the active forces who were home on leave. He had on occasions taught some subject in which he was an hour ahead of his class and had said to them, 'We will work together and worry through it somehow.' Now, however, he was supposed to know his book, but once unfortunately when he was addressing his troop, the major came along and said, 'Haven't you got it up?' This was rather hard after his experience at the College, where teacher and student learnt together.

Sir Everard im Thurn, the distinguished guest of the evening, in returning thanks for the toast of 'the guests', told of many interesting incidents in his recent trip to Australia with Sir Charles Lucas and Professor Kirkaldy. What he described as 'the finest thing he had ever seen' was 'the intense eagerness of the Australians to join in with the mother country over the war', of which Sir Charles contrived to make very full use. Talking of the lighter side when the Lascars (Indian stewards and sailors) on board (the ship that was carrying them home) refused to go farther than Bombay, and practically all the passengers signed on as deck-hands, the zeal of Sir Charles became very pronounced. They 'did not mind so much if he turned the hose-pipe on himself, but when he turned it on to other people, it became necessary to suggest to him that he was of a fit age for some other quiet employment.'

Old Students' Supper, December 18th, 1915

The account of this supper shows vividly the difference in material conditions in the early stages of the First World War, compared to conditions in 1939-40.

It was still possible in 1915 to seat and feed 138 guests 'on whom the College portraits looked down from their accustomed places'. The supper was held at the early hour of 6.30 in the

* Another brilliant teacher, later killed in action in Palestine.

OLD STUDENTS' SUPPERS AND TEAS 1914-18

coffee- and common-room instead of the Maurice Hall, which was fully occupied as the recruiting hall for the St Pancras Rifles. . . . College men acted as waiters, the fare provided was 'slightly more simple than of yore and the celebrated "Tansley Punch" was conspicuous by its absence'. The Chairman proposing the toast of the College said 'it needed all the good wishes and support we could give it'. A 'Message of goodwill' from the 'only surviving Founder,' the Rev. Llewelyn Davies, was read out: and one of regret for being unable to attend from 'our late Principal', Professor Dicey, who enclosed £1 for the Furnivall Collection for Children.

The Chairman and Sir Charles Lucas made enormous long speeches. 'The College is carrying on in spite of its many difficulties.' 'Let us be neither unduly elated by success nor cast down by misfortune' and similar comments that to modern ears are clichés, abounded. These remarks are quoted, not in a spirit of mockery, but to show that what was completely acceptable to one generation, produced an entirely different reaction in a later age. 'Proud as I am,' Sir Charles Lucas opens his speech by observing, 'at all times to have my name connected with the College, I feel more pride in speaking for it at a time of crisis faced manfully and well, than in the easy days of prosperity and peace.' Sometimes one is tempted to think that the inhibitions of those earlier days, mainly associated with 'the proprieties', were preferable to the modern horror of putting into words thoughts that spring from the emotions. Sir Charles was capable also of a lighter touch. 'Our thoughts go out to our brethren at the front, and the Marks Fellowship is determined that if they can help it, they shall not come back as "returned empties", but that they shall come back with full stomachs as well as with full hearts. . . . Mr Weller described "funds" as "things that go up and down in the city", but the Comforts Fund, or its result, is something that goes down in the trenches. The men in the trenches are good trenchermen and I like to think of them enjoying the contents of their parcels and lighting up their cigarettes to the tune of "The Old Smokes at Home". . . . Turning to the Home Department,' he continued, 'our classes are more or less skeleton classes, but there are no skeletons in our cupboard, nor is our cupboard bare. We have food for mind and body. Where could you produce such skeletons as our Vice-Principal (Lupton) or Mr Dent (Chairman Old Students' Club) and Mr (Alexander) Hepburn? . . . Surely they might be labelled as "worn yet plump" and are ocular demonstrations that in war as well as in peace the College produces "all round men".' There is more in the same vein of bantering humour; and puns, today an outmoded form of fun, abound. But the speaker ends on a serious, indeed almost a Churchillian note: 'There can be no compromise . . . we must fight on till right prevails over might . . . but in doing so, let us bear in mind Abraham Lincoln's noble words. "With malice towards none, with charity for all, with firmness in the right as God gives us to see the right." Gentlemen, I say that it is in this spirit that we and our College will face whatever is coming to us next year.'

Sir Charles Lucas was followed by the Chairman, J. J. Dent, who proposed the toast of 'the Guests'. 'Friends,' he said, 'in changing our constitution recently, the College decided to bring into our work a number of labour organizations, among them the Workers' Educational Association, and tonight we have with us its President, The Rev. W. Temple; the late Secretary, Albert Mansbridge; and Goodman, the Secretary of the London Branch. . . . The Club and Institute Union is represented by Mr Jesse Argyle, who is also a worker in the W.E.A. and we are glad to welcome him here tonight. Mr A. Hainsworth is here for the Co-operative Union, and he has shown his enthusiasm during his short life on our College Council not only by inducing his organization to give us a handsome donation, but also by becoming a generous subscriber himself. We have also to welcome representatives of two other organizations, the St. Pancras Labour Representation Committee, and the London Trades Council, the members of which we are anxious to get here, to spread the influence of the College. Then there is another type of organization, the London County Council, represented by Inspector Mr Beresford Ingram, and we hope he will be well satisfied with us.

'Of Mr Pett Ridge (the guest of the evening) surely it would be presumption on my part to say much. He is a good friend to the College and he is a good friend to the poor of the locality, into whose lives he has a great and sympathetic insight. Another old friend is our architect Mr W. D. Caroe. Few men there are, outside of those we call ourselves, who have done so much for the College as he. I recollect many years ago, on the strength of a very slight acquaintance, asking him with the impertinence of youth if he would undertake the difficult and troublesome job of turning our old place in Great Ormond Street into a handsome College, without any prospect of pay for doing it. He at once consented, and in such a way as to make me think I was conferring a favour on him by asking him. The latest instance of his kindness is the designing of the new Library shelving, which our friend, A. A. Pegram (College Student, by profession a cabinet maker) has so splendidly carried out.'

This account in the *Journal* of the Old Students' Supper of 1915 highlights some interesting trends of that time.

Mr Pett Ridge was then a popular contemporary novelist, and through his novels, a sympathetic chronicler of the lives of humble folk. Today it would be hard to find one of his works in a secondhand bookshop.

Dent's reference to him as 'a good friend to the poor of this locality' rings like an echo from a Victorian preacher. But indeed it is not so distant as that. I can recall between the wars on the occasion of the Children's Furnival Treat – a magnificent tea-party – the pathetic queue of little ones, often coatless, in their best frocks, waiting in the bitter cold for the doors to open; the tail of the queue, most pitiful of all, consisting of those who had not had the good fortune to be invited, but were still desperately hoping to get in. (They usually did.) The qualification for admission was poverty. Invitations were given to the local schools, and the teachers asked to select the children from the poorest families, to receive them. The lure was games in the gymnasium (usually led by Brandt, who was a schoolmaster), a vast tea, a toy, a garment, and a new minted penny from Father Christmas – a Scots Father Christmas, Alexander Hepburn, beaming and magnificent in flowing white beard and scarlet robe. To the slum children of Camden Town this was pure fairyland; it would probably be despised by their more sophisticated, and prosperous descendants today. One is thankful for the comparative disappearance of poverty, but less certain about the benefits of modern sophistication.

Another point of interest in Dent's speech concerns the 'new trend' to invite numerous outside bodies to be represented on the College Council.

OLD STUDENTS' SUPPERS AND TEAS 1914-18

In the rewriting of the Constitution in 1963 (for reasons that do not concern this chronicle) the innovation, so proudly recorded by Dent in 1915, was, after prolonged discussion, deliberately reversed, and the number of such bodies having the right to be represented on the Council was notably reduced.

In 1916 both the Old Folks' and the Children's Treats took place. The Maurice Hall having been requisitioned for war purposes, on the latter occasion 'only 198 children were present!'

There were no Furnival Treats during the Second World War, old people and children having, officially, been evacuated from London, as a part of air raid precautions.

The fortieth annual supper of the Old Students' Club was held on December 16th, 1916, in the common-room and coffee-room, eighty-seven members and guests being seated.

Leonard Pocock, President of the Club, proposed the toast of the College, remarking 'the outstanding event of the year in the history of the College – apart from the war – has been the death of the Rev. Llewelyn Davies the last survivor of our founders – aged 90. It has been my good fortune to know six of the Founders. . . . I . . . ask you to remember these men and their spirit in connection with the toast of the College at this time, because of the great importance of preserving, as far as in us lies . . . the continuity of the work they began . . . and the spirit running through it all. I speak as an Old Student. . . . All of them (the founders) worked in this College for the love of the work and of their fellow men, gladly learning and gladly teaching . . . it is as wise as it is a fundamental rule of the College that a man joining it to partake of its many benefits must be a student *first* – he must join a class as a condition of his membership – a student first, a club man second – new students who join here for the first time mostly join a class in some subject which they expect will be a help to them in earning their living. The College does not discourage men from so joining for a utilitarian purpose . . . but it does commend and extol the pursuit of higher subjects – the humanities, history, literature, languages and so on – the pursuit of knowledge for its own sake. . . .'

These remarks are so fundamental to the College still today, they seemed worth setting out fully here. The rest of the speech

OLD STUDENTS' SUPPERS AND TEAS 1914-18

was full of wisdom and serious comment on the war and the ideals for which we were fighting, and of grave references to our losses.

He was followed by Lucas, who responded for the College, and by Lupton, who gave the toast of 'Our Founders' and finally by 'Major-General Maurice', the theme of whose speech was 'cheerfulness'. He spoke of the men at the front, and of those wounded and maimed in the hospitals. 'The characteristic which strikes everyone upon seeing our forces abroad is their cheerfulness. . . . This College has a right to be cheerful for it has done its duty, sending out its full tale of numbers. . . . You have taught our men to "set the cause above renown, to love the game above the prize, to honour when they strike him down, the foe that comes with fearless eyes" . . .' There were more toasts and speeches, Lionel Jacob for the guests, C. G. Cash for the Marks Fellowship and Old Students' Club, coupled with the names of Alexander Hepburn and Charles Wright. Hepburn responded – an alarmingly full measure of speeches!

Old Students' Tea, 1917

By December 1917, the long strain of war, and the problems arising from the fairly strict food rationing that had been introduced at a late stage of the war, would make catering for a major meal for large numbers extremely difficult. There had also been air raids on London, insignificant by comparison with the attacks suffered in the Second World War, but a new and terrifying experience then. It was probably for these reasons that, rather surprisingly, we read in the *Journal* 'what an excellent idea of Mrs Lionel Jacob's it was to have a tea instead of a supper on December 15th, and the result fully justified the change. A supper would not have been nearly so popular; as it was twelve dozen sat down to table, including a number of young students who embraced the opportunity, and thus became introduced to the College spirit manifested at these annual gatherings of the Old Students' Club. We had the pleasure of seeing Major-General Frederick Maurice, of the Army Council, the grandson of our Founder, who brought with him his son Frederick, and who also made a most excellent and heartening speech. Our Principal, Sir Charles Lucas, again gave a splendid address, and the meeting as a whole was a great success –

OLD STUDENTS' SUPPERS AND TEAS 1914-18

greater than might have been thought possible in the case of the fourth held since the war began. As it was a tea, the toasts had to be "dry", but we should like to congratulate Mrs Simmons and her staff on the way the tea was served, and our thanks are due to all who helped to make it a purely College affair, and to enable us to dispense with any outside assistance.'

Many of the Principal's speeches have already been quoted in these pages – it is not therefore proposed to give a full account here of what was said on this occasion. Certain of his remarks however have an interest still today. First of these is an item of domestic information – 'The Executive decided,' Sir Charles said, 'and I think wisely, not to hold Founders' Day this year (1917), and not to have an Old Students' Supper. This gathering is a kind of compromise between the two. We do not aspire to the stern seriousness of Founders' Day, and we fall short of the buoyant exuberance of the Old Students' Supper. This is a mild compromise, and we call it "the college small and early". As the war has gone on the College has become smaller and earlier. It is becoming small by degrees, and beautifully less, and beautifully is the right word. . . . I for one delight that our numbers are depleted through members of the College answering the call of duty and the call of honour.

'The College is becoming earlier from a reason that commonly conduces to early hours, that is "change of air", and because of certain doubtful blessings that are showered upon us from above. . . .'

Lucas in the course of the speech refers to the recent death of Lord Grey. . . . 'He had two passions in his life, one was the British Empire which he thought, as I think, had unbounded potency for good; the other was ennobling the lives of the working-classes in this country . . .' The speaker concluded with a moving reference to the ideals for which the College stands, and to the students who had given their lives in the fight. He speaks of 'the Founders who set before us a light unto our path . . . not the interest of man or of class, but of duty to and responsibility for others. . . . We learnt the lesson anew from sons of the College who gave their lives for men.'

A collection was made for the Furnivall Treats.

After Lionel Jacob had proposed the toast of 'College men at the front', Major General Maurice spoke, principally on the progress of the war; a strong speech, full of encouragement and confidence. A speech from Charles Wright, commendably brief, brought the orations to a close.

There was another Old Students' Tea in 1918, the last of the series. Lucas made use of the occasion to welcome back to the College Harold Pocock, son of the Chairman of the Marks Fellowship, repatriated from a prisoner-of-war camp. Another College prisoner recently repatriated was Simmons the caretaker, whose wife had gallantly carried on with their joint duties throughout the years of his absence.

In his speech which was long, and serious in purpose, but lightened with the occasional humorous comment that was typical of the speaker, Lucas referred to the returned prisoners of war, particularly Harold Pocock. 'None,' he said, 'would for a moment compare our returned prisoners of war to Prodigal Sons, but some of them in a strange country would "fain have filled their bellies with the husks that the swine did eat". They are not quite so fortunate in their return as the Prodigal Son, as you could not possibly scrape enough coupons together to make a fatted calf. . . .'

Major-General Sir Frederick Maurice returning thanks said: 'I have only been back from France a few hours. In fact I got up at five this morning and motored nine miles to catch the early boat in order to have the pleasure of being here this evening. . . . I have been motoring some 2,000 miles between Dixmude and the Vosge. I went over the whole of the ground on which our last great advance, and our final victories and the war were won. . . . The difficulties that faced our men were incomparably greater than at any other part of the line, yet they did more than either the French or the Americans. . . . The part they are now playing in Germany is as honourable as, and not very much easier, than the part they played in France. They are behaving with a dignity and restraint altogether admirable. . . .'

Maurice then explained the difficulties of 'supply transport and demobilization then existing . . .' There were numerous other speeches by members of the College before the guests got down to having tea. . . . In 1919 The Old Students' Suppers were resumed.

IX

LETTERS FROM THE HOME FRONT

HERE, written in November 1917, is a letter from the Home Front, where air raids on civilian objectives were a new feature of the war.

The College Spirit and Air Raids, November 1917
'As the present writer's last mouthful of College pudding was passing along its appointed course, the Superintendent announced that the "Take Cover" warning had been given. At once the members of the public who were waiting outside the College were allowed to enter, so far as accommodation was available, and were given the eastern end of the basement and ground-floor corridors, the western end being reserved for College members and their friends. Altogether they numbered some 350. The ringing of the College bell summoned the classes to depart from their labours, and shelter in the allotted places. Everything was done in order, and the arrangements, organized and supervised by three of our "Specials" (i.e. special constables) A. H. Perry, Hepburn, and Dimes, worked with the utmost smoothness. The old College veterans remained in the common-room until the guns began to fire. Then most of them retired, quietly and in good order, to the corridor, but some stalwarts remained in their armchairs, although the lights in the room were turned off, and only a glimmer was given by the night-light which now burns in the hearth, for the discomfiture of match profiteers. From the basement came the sounds of a

concert, at first solos of quite excellent quality, and then, as the guns began to bark, "something with a chorus", which, as violent and prolonged outbursts of shrapnel exploded overhead, swelled to the full extent of the lungs of the audience, who were out to show that they could drown the combined sound of bombs and guns. When at last this "first round" was over, silence such as London never knew before succeeded. The streets were empty of people, all of whom had taken cover. A line of deserted tramcars, with all lights out except the police lights, were ranged along Crowndale Road, their drivers and lady conductors having chosen the College as a place of refuge. Even the canary which, secure in its cage tied round with a big red handkerchief, is brought nightly to the College as soon as the doors are open to the public, found its thoughts too deep for song. So passed a long time, broken with fitful outbursts of gunfire. From time to time the chorus in the basement struck up again, varied on one occasion with the appropriate if premature refrain of "The end of a perfect day".

'Our "specials", whose uniform gave a pleasing sense of complete safety to all, brought round cans of water for the watchers, and for the floor some fearsome compound (fetched by Perry from the laboratory during the firing) a compound which mightily overcame the heat and "fog". Then, after some two hours, there came the last and heaviest outburst, this time with a new note which we could not recognize as that of any of our old friends, guns or bombs. Later we found it to be the voice of a mobile gun which had come to anchor in Oakley Square. So ended the longest aeroplane raid we had experienced for soon after, all the lights were turned on both in and out of the College, the tram drivers and conductors went back and drove off their trams; the public, flocking into the streets from all the neighbouring "funk-holes", sent up a cheer that another raid was over, and but little harm done; and Frances and Lucy (the serving-room girls) and the others did a brisk trade in cocoa and coffee, though many of the stalwarts sighed to think that the supplies of beer had run short days ago.

'This short sketch of how the College spirit grappled with the new problem of air raids, may be of interest to readers in after time, when the war with all its horrors is over. . . . The College classes must inevitably suffer as the result of so very disturbed a week at the very opening of the new College year. But as far as possible the disturbance to the College has been reduced to a minimum. The Shakespeare readers . . . continued and completed their appointed reading in defiance of bombs and guns, the only change being they occupied the safest part of the basement in lieu of their ordinary room. So, on the Tuesday, as soon as the "All Clear" signal had been given, the Executive tackled its long agenda, and the attendance was fully up to average. On the day following the last of the raids, there was mingled with the sense of relief, some feeling of disappointment that we had to go home without having had our nightly dose of excitement . . .'

The article is signed A.S.L.; the initials of the Vice-Principal, Arthur S. Lupton.

*   *   *   *   *

'Thus conscience doth make cowards of us all.' Bernard Pitt was assuredly no coward, but his conscience seems to have troubled him in an odd way at the moment of his country's need.

Second Lieut. Bernard Pitt, 3rd Battn., the Border Regt., Shoeburyness, 10th April, 1915.

'I was immensely pleased and not a little humbled by the letter the class sent me. I feel so glad that my desertion of the College, which caused me so many doubts and misgivings, was not felt as a desertion, but only as a return to that allegiance which comes before all, and to which the College itself is in fealty, the cause of the Nation. I have sent the letter to my wife to keep for me, for I shall be bandied about the country like a football. Who can tell though? I may be kept here, or I may go to Chatham for an entrenchment course. One thing, whatever happens, we do what we are told, we go and come, and thank God for any odd mercies which are bestowed on us. When I get a reasonable lump of leave, I shall come up to the College. Give my love to all and tell them how glad I am that the College has kept together.'

Bernard Pitt fought in France and was killed in action. Another tragedy for the College, for he was one of the young men of great promise with the capacity for leadership.

X

SOME LETTERS FROM THE ROYAL NAVY

SOME of the letters from men serving in the Royal Navy in 1915–16 make College history.

The letters written during the Second World War have nothing comparable to the account of King George V's visit to H.M.S. *Antrim*, or the formidable list of great personages, including Lord Kitchener, carried in H.M.S. *Dartmouth*.

The Russian decoration bestowed on N. H. Pether was a rare distinction. The 'sailor's eye' view of the Battle of Jutland has a flavour that the official history of that battle does not wholly confirm, while the factual description of the launching of an aeroplane from a ship at Felixstowe in preparation for an attack on the enemy, reads like a comic strip – and one would marvel at the author's invention!

From Mech. D. F. Bowering, R.N. Air Service, Felixstowe, July/15.

'The *Journal* again delighted me when I received same a few days ago, it having been forwarded on from the ship to which I belong. I am always pleased to receive the *Journal* and to know how the College progresses and of its doings.

'Perhaps you will be interested in the following little incident that occurred to me whilst we were preparing for an air raid on the German Coast. It is necessary for a mechanic to go with the pilot in the machine whilst launching same from the ship, which is proceeding at anything from eighteen to twenty knots. The machine having been launched by means of a crane over the stern of the ship, I proceeded to start the engine going. As the Admiralty only allows the pilot to proceed on these dangerous missions, the mechanic has to find his best way to the ship by swimming. So I waited for the signal to dive, when the machine suddenly left the water and threw me overboard from a height of about fifteen feet. When I recovered from the shock I found the ship still steaming away, and myself struggling in the sea. However, being a fairly good swimmer I managed to keep afloat, despite the heavy sea running and of course my clothes saturated. On these occasions one thinks of anything but the right thing, and I found myself thinking of submarines and Zeppelins and a host of other ugly things. But I was greatly relieved when, after having swum quite 300 to 350 yards, I found the ship's motor-boat by my side. Am glad to say, after a couple of days' rest and some of the ship's grog, I am quite well again and longing for the next excitement.'

From Assist. Paymaster J. W. Horsley, H.M.S. *Antrim*, Third Cruiser Squadron, Grand Fleet, 1915.

'I am afraid little attention is paid to the so-called "submarine blockade", because I think it is practically all bluff, though they seem to bag a slow ship now and again. A fast ship can easily out-manœuvre our diving friends. We have not had any excitement since the *Blücher* stunt* : that was an anxious and exciting day for us, and quite an experience for me. However, we get some very dangerous jobs at times, and never know what is going to happen next. Last week was very bad weather at sea, washing us down, flooding cabins and turning us topsy-turvy. On Saturday last, while we were in the midst of coaling, the King (King George V) paid us a visit. He caught us on the hop and came into the ward-room with the remains of lunch on the

---

* The *Blücher* was sunk in the Battle of the Dogger Bank in January 1915. It was an ill-fated name in the German Navy, for in 1940 a battleship of the same name was sunk by Norwegian shore batteries during the invasion of Norway.

table. He seemed very pleased and said it reminded him of his time in the Navy.'

The Battle of Jutland

Musician Evans 'was privileged . . . to go through the Battle of Jutland,' he writes on June 12th, 1916. 'Many thanks for the *Journal*, which as you know, is always welcome and coming as it did after our great fight, when one needs rest and something pleasant. . . . Our ship was in it from the first. . . . I was bemoaning my fate at having to keep afternoon drill, after the morning's drill, but of course that is all in the game . . . when I heard a tramping and rushing, and remarked that I believed action stations had been sounded. In a few seconds all the men with me were in their places, and the usual orders passed . . . at about 4.30 word came that [names, unfortunately were censored] had sighted smoke, as from a large fleet, on the horizon . . . we gave a cheer at the prospect of at last showing the enemy what our ships were made of . . . in five minutes . . . —— [for security reasons there occurs here a blank or rather, censor's blot out, in the letter] was engaging the enemy. We all steeled our nerves for what was ahead of us. . . . Our officer gave us some cheering words, and the order came to load with position range, and we opened fire at about 20,000 yards. . . . Closing in, with orders continually passing, the battle lasted about an hour . . . we were giving the *Hindenburg* a taste of our big shells, then we turned out attention to the *Denzlmeer*, and next had a pot at a ship called the *Kaiser*, and I can assure you that if either of them returned to port, they will never fight again. Of course we did not get off without a scratch, we were rather badly mauled inboard, but we remained a fighting unit till the last. The Germans had about thirty or more ships, or easily three to one . . . before the Grand Fleet came up. We gave them three cheers, but the Germans made off* as soon as they sighted them, chased by our destroyers which played havoc with the remnants of their fleet . . . by the next morning there was not much left of what was once the German Fleet. Before I close I must say that one of the finest men to wear the uniform is our Admiral . . .'

* The flight of the German ships before the Grand Fleet is historically correct.

LETTERS FROM THE ROYAL NAVY

From S.S.A., N. H. Pether, writer, R.N., H.M.S. *Jupiter*, April 17, 1915.

'Ice and snow has been our motto for two months, experiencing terrible gales at times, but by jove now the climate is A1. The sun shines brightly nearly all day, rising about 3 a.m. setting about 9 p.m. only on one occasion in rough weather did I not wish to die. Bread and jam and bread alone has been my meals on most Sundays since the end of February, but how glad I am I came to experience such a time.

'Expect a European war map from me, printed in Russian, for the benefit of fellow students.'

From N. H. Pether, Writer, R.N. Devonport, 12th May, 1916.

'H.M. The Emperor of Russia has conferred on me the Russian silver medal "for Zeal" with the Ribbon of the Order of St Stanislaus, for duty when in Russia between February and May 1915, whilst in H.M.S. *Jupiter*. H.M. the King is graciously pleased to grant permission to wear this decoration on all occasions. Announced in the Press 24th April and myself missing it, I had no idea I had been honoured till my uncle showed me a cutting on the following Wednesday.

'The decoration was founded originally on a Polish order by Stanislaus Augustus Goniatowski in 1765 and adopted as a Russian order in 1831.'

From S.S.A., N. H. Pether, Writer, R.N., H.M.S. *Dartmouth* 8.12.1916.

'Many thanks for College *Journal* received today. It is pleasant to know the welfare of the College from month to month, the progress of the war in the eyes of its members. The personal letters make very nice reading, giving one a broader view of what really occurs in the zone of war.

'Although a small boat, carrying about 450 men, and a good fighting calibre she (his ship, the *Dartmouth*) has done her bit. Many celebrities have taken passage in her including Earl Kitchener when he left Marseilles for Egypt, Salonica, Gallipoli, to return to Naples on his way to Rome. When at Piraeus he was only absent from the ship for about two hours on his visit to King Constantine and it was only after the interview the stringent blockade on Greece was released. K of K was a great personality with eyes that glared through one, but his secretary Fitzgerald overruled him. Often one could hear Fitzgerald thundering away at K of K giving sound advice, often at times both tempers were elevated, yet they remained two great pals.

'The *Dartmouth* had the honour of carrying many others including the C. of the Forces at Alonika, General Sarrail, General Horne, Marshal Patrick, The Serbian C. in Chief, General Maxwell late C. in Chief in Egypt and Ireland, General Birdwood, the Anzac, and the King of Montenegro.'

Second Lieut. A. E. Homewood, Royal Engineers, B.M.E.F., writing home on and after 8th September, 1915, says:

'Here we are, fairly settled to the routine of shipboard. She is a fine, steady old barge, if slow, and the weather so far has been from fairly smooth to oily smooth. A fair number of the men have been queer, but so far I have done justice to the ship's admirable cookery, even if it did take an effort yesterday morning. It is beginning to be very warm o' nights especially when the ports are closed and darkened, and I am wearing a light coat. It was so funny last night to leave the pleasant, pretty drawing-room – exactly like that of an hotel ashore, save that the ceiling is a bit low – dainty as possible, with a young officer tinkling softly but well on the piano, and captains and majors playing bridge, and step out to the darkness and silence of the deck, past the dimly seen forms of the sentries, and listen to the surge of the water and watch the phosphorescent light on the waves. The night was full of the most wonderful stars, and I had time to ruminate and try to grasp it all. And I thought very much of home.

'This strange floating town, all alone in mid ocean! Smart young officers, and young officers who are evidently not smart. The O.C. troops is a fine-looking major, about the handsomest man aboard, with moustache to match. And we have some curiously antique dugouts, and some awfully nice boys. . . . Troops with half the geography of England in their names, and a gang of the roughest, dirtiest, old Irish boys you can imagine. And I've got half a dozen officers, including a captain and a full lieutenant, to help me at alarm drill. For that is the shadow that lies across us. Had not the Devil invented submarines, this would have been a perfect pleasure trip. . . . We practise, but if the *real thing* happened – well – say it reverently and with intent, God help us! . . . Did I tell you what a send-off we got when we left port? The boys of the training ships manned the yards and rigging, and cheered like mad. Bugles blew from the camps ashore, steamers sounded their sirens, and the green shores of the river looked as lovely as the queen of counties always looks. Some day I shall write the Odyssey of this voyage. Gib, as we saw it, might have been Southend or any old place. We have lurched through the Mediterranean on an erratic course, and this morning I awoke to find strange khaki-coloured shores sliding past the port-hole, between the blue sky and the bluer sea.'

Although not from an officer of the Royal Navy, this letter describes a naval occasion, and thus would seem to take its place alongside the letters from the Royal Navy.

XI

LETTERS FROM THE B.E.F., FRANCE

FROM Brigadier-General Frederick Maurice, C.B., General H.Q., British Army in the Field, June 6th, 1916.

We make no apology for putting General Maurice's letter at the head of all the letters received from France. Not only did he play a distinguished part in the war, but he became Principal of the College afterwards.

After acknowledging receipt of the *Journal*, and enclosing 'a small contribution to wipe off the deficit in its accounts,' he continues, 'I am very glad to see that the College is well represented here. . . . We want every man, every round of ammunition, and all the help we can get. . . . It is wonderfully impressive out here to see the quiet, ungrudging and wholehearted sacrifice France is making. We are fighting on a fifty mile front, and the French on a front nine times as long, yet we never hear any talk of French casualties. Multiply ours nine times, and you can imagine what theirs are. The almost universal black of the women's dresses is the only sign of them. . . . Thank God our women and children have been spared the horrors many of theirs have gone through. It is perhaps not easy to realize that by fighting out here in a foreign country we are defending our hearths and homes, and all that is dear to us, but it is so. . . . Many thanks for your kindly reference to myself. The College is very dear to me.'

It is interesting to watch, in the pages of the *Journal*, Maurice's progress in the military hierarchy. The first reference is to Lieut.-Colonel Maurice.

Private E. Hulls, R.A.M.C., whose letter is post-marked 'Field Post Office' writes 5th February, 1915, from France.
'I thank you for the *Journal* received yesterday evening. Such was my eagerness to read something English that I took it with me to the firing-line in the wee, sma' hours. Sometimes we have to wait for an opportunity to move the wounded, and on this occasion I had time to read your very interesting account of the "supper". My "Common Room" was an almost demolished cottage and a flickering candle. Once it almost seemed falling from the vibration of a shell bursting near us. I smiled when I thought of the comparative luxury of your water toast.* Here, although we chlorinate the water and then boil it, we take it very much like a dose of salts. But that is not to be wondered at when one sees the awful carnage throughout the town. And we realize that we must be bold to carry on this grim business against a very determined enemy. Nevertheless, we are all "merry and bright",† and in this vein I renew my good wishes to the College.'

Pte. Thomas Darvell, Machine-Gun Section, 3rd Battn., London Regt., T.F., B.E.F. France, relates his experiences in the terrible battle of Neuve Chapelle in 1916.
'Thank you very much for the College *Journal*, which I was delighted to receive, giving me welcome news of the College. I see my name is down in the list of students believed to be in the fighting zone. Have you heard of the part taken by the 3rd Royal Fusiliers in the battle of Neuve Chapelle? Being in the Machine-Gun Section, I was right up amongst it, and it was a sight I never wish to see again. I will try to describe the battle. First of all we had orders that we were to go into the trenches the night before; that a bombardment was to take place next day, and that we were to take the village. We had rather a quiet night, just a few shots exchanged and a few shells whizzing overhead.

* On the occasion referred to no alcohol was provided at the supper, whether because none was to be had, or as a gesture of patriotic restraint, is not related.

† A quotation from a popular song of that time.

Just before the time fixed for the bombardment everything seemed quiet and we were full of excitement. On the very stroke of the minute, the bombardment started. There was a terrific din; hell seemed to have been let loose. Looking over the top of the trench you could see the shells bursting. The guns seemed to be like one huge machine-gun, the bigger ones making a louder explosion. After ten minutes' firing the excitement was intense, trenches were being blown sky high, Germans going up as well. And as they were retiring machine-guns cut them down in hundreds. Then came the charge. Believe me this was the most exciting point in the battle, the men charging like demons. Some of the Germans were so frightened that they threw down their arms and ran towards us. You would have laughed to see about a hundred hefty Germans being chased by a little Gurkha towards our own trenches. During the attack our men were falling right and left, but the Germans lost more than we. Well, we captured the village and the Germans retired into some woods about a thousand yards beyond it. . . . The Germans did not counter-attack that day on our section of the line, but tried to on the left of us. . . . As it happened the attack came off on the morning after, the day between being spent in repairing the captured trenches. The night before the counter attack I snatched a few minutes' sleep. I was not allowed to rest long, for quickly came the order to "stand to", Germans attacking. The dawn was just breaking. Looking over the top of the trench I could see what appeared to be figures moving towards us, and it turned out to be Germans advancing in massed formation. We immediately opened a murderous fire with machine-guns and rifles. Nothing could stand against it. Again and again they attacked, but they were repulsed each time, leaving hundreds of dead behind them. I must say our fellows behaved wonderfully well during the whole affair, even making jokes while they were firing, no doubt in consequence of the great victory in which they had taken part.'

We paid a heavy price for the 'victory' at Neuve Chapelle. But the advance clearly put new heart into the soldiers.

It is strange, among such grim and stirring reports, to find this *Editorial* Note.

LETTERS FROM THE B.E.F., FRANCE

'The Editor would be much obliged if those readers who are serving with the forces would kindly acknowledge receipt of this month's *Journal* when it reaches them, so that he may know whether the copies posted go astray or duly arrive at their intended destinations.'

May 1916.

Qmr. Sergt. F. C. Fischer, Canteen, H.Q. 56th Division, B.E.F., writes April 13th, 1916.

'Dear Comrades, Thanks very much for your jolly handy parcel. I have a fine chance of seeing many of the College members out here, as I am in charge of a Division Canteen, the Division being composed of Londoners. I have just left a Division where I knew everyone and they were all very pally. Of course it is not the same as being in the trenches, but we have our anxious times, if you can call them such. After I was wounded, and also after I was put as medically unfit, I came to take charge of a canteen, which had not then a halfpenny capital, but when I left, it had many thousand francs capital. So you see we have done good work among our own men. All their profit is returned to them by our providing theatres and buying a cinematograph and everything that is wanted for their comfort. I enjoy the work very much indeed, as I am always right up with the men wherever they go. I have just come out of a large city, very much knocked about by the Germans. As usual, and as at Ypres, where I was before, the Cathedral and other large buildings have caught it most. The foe are only a thousand yards off, and often send a few shells into the town. One gets used to this, like the civilians do. There are still 800 left and they live in the cellars. Good luck, boys! I am still alive and merry, after eighteen months out here.'

Sous Officier Trape taught French at the College. This letter, typical of a Frenchman, is one of a number he wrote to the College. Headed 'March 23rd by Moonlight. *Des Tranche ou ça barde*,' it describes how the writer is 'on the front again for the third time. Now I am used to it. I go to the advance trenches as easily as I should go home. . . . In our army the chiefs rely on the chasseurs [he was a chasseur] for the defence and the attack, and for that reason our *corps d'élite* are always admirably placed.

LETTERS FROM THE B.E.F., FRANCE

We can nearly touch with our fingers the actors on the adverse stage. The College *Journal*, for which I thank you. . . . I peruse it with delight . . . by this link I keep touch with you all, who are my friends . . .'

One is glad to be able to report that Sous Officier Trape came safely through the war.

The letter printed below was written from a training camp in England. But it ties up with Grugeon's first letter from France, and for that reason has its place here.

1915. Private Arthur Grugeon, 'C' Co., 15th County of London, Dorking.

'Today we have been for a battalion route-march. We started at 9 and kept on till 3, with only 10 minutes' halt every hour and half-an-hour for our ration. We are in rather hilly country, and consequently I am about dead tired. I am billeted in an empty house and am fairly comfortable. I sleep on the floor and have three blankets for my bed. I have got in a supply of coal, etc., so enjoy a fire, keep thoroughly warm, and find it most convenient for drying clothes when wet through – often the case lately. Please give my regards to *all*.'

From the same – France, 1915.

'We had no sleep whilst travelling, although it took three days and nights. The boat was packed, and we were like sardines, and the train was worse. In France the soldiers do not travel in carriages, but in ordinary trucks. We had fifty in ours, and there wasn't even room to lie down. We had to sit on our packs or stand up to avoid cramp. We were in that position for twenty-two hours, and then marched for ten miles over cobble-stones. By that time we were absolutely done up, and could only go straight to sleep. . . . We all had a pair of socks given us, and a note from Queen Mary. . . . We are billeted in farm-houses, and sleep in barns in straw. We share beds with all sorts of things. First a cow wakes us, then a horse or some chickens. . . . This will be a funny Easter for me. . . . Have been under fire for the first time today, and jolly good sport it is. Shells burst over us as we were marching along the canal, but no harm was done. . . .

I am writing this amid shot and shell. We are in the firing trench and the Germans are only about one hundred yards away. Just at the moment we are under terrific shellfire, and it is awfully exciting watching them burst. We keep being covered with mud and dust, but that is nothing. It is impossible to keep clean, but it is very amusing.'

April 1915.
'Many thanks for the *Journal*, which I received safely and digested amidst shot and shell in the trenches. . . . We are now fully-fledged soldiers and have ourselves held a stretch of trenches that were only seventy yards from the Germans. I am enjoying it all immensely, but am looking forward to returning home to England. Now that the weather is drying up and the trenches are quite clean, we ought to be getting a move on, and I hope to be in the front when we do start. Please remember me to *all*. . . .'

Sergt. Cyril H. Bowes, D. Co., West Riding Regt., B.E.F. 27th August, 1915.
"I had an exciting experience the other morning. It was very misty early, so we took the opportunity to go and look at the barbed wire, which badly needed repair. While four of us were busily engaged mending it, the mist rose and we were discovered in all our glory twenty yards in front of our trench and within forty of the enemy, who were ungentlemanly enough to turn a machine-gun on us. We lay low until the fire slackened a bit and then bolted for home, getting back without a scratch, which was lucky. Some of the boys bear charmed lives. The Huns put out a blue and white flag, and a sergeant and private from the battalion on our right went out *in broad daylight* and brought it in! I am feeling fit, but life in the trenches is a great strain in more ways than one. Kindest regards to all.'

From: Sergt F. O. Wright, 13.12.1916.
'Very many thanks for parcel received quite safely. I hope these few lines will find you and all at the College in the best of health as it leaves me feeling in the pink at present. I receive the *Journal* every month and it comes very acceptable indeed as it recalls many pleasant times spent at the old College in bygone

days, but us all hopes to meet there again in the near future. But I notice that through the losses the number of College men is getting smaller every day.'

This, as any officer who was unfortunate enough to be employed in censoring letters would know, is a typical 'Tommy's' effort. They were all in 1914 hoping their correspondents were 'feeling in the pink as it leaves me at present'. For that reason and because of its nostalgic reference to the College, it is reproduced now.

From Lieut. Bernard Pitt to Lionel Jacob.
'I am now in a hilly wooded region like the skirts of the Kentish Downs, with copses full of anemones . . . the ground round about is poisoned with human relics, limbs and bundles of clothes . . . even those poor remains of men which pious hands have buried, are daily disinterred by plunging shells. . . . Do you wonder that reading Wordsworth this afternoon in a clearing of the unpolluted woods. . . . I felt a disgust even to sickness of the appalling wickedness of war? Sometimes one has great need of a strength that is not in one's power to use, but is a grace of God. I have seen very heavy fighting in different parts of our line . . .
'I was recommended for the Military Cross, but my usual bad luck intervened to relegate me to mentioned in despatches only. . . . Now I am in command of a trench mortar battery and I find the work as interesting as any war-making can be.'

Pitt had evidently the soul of a poet. He was killed in a mine explosion in the trenches. His commanding officer sent a letter to his wife full of praises for his many fine qualities of leadership, and his great bravery.
The letter printed above is the writing of a highly sensitive man. Realizing this adds considerable weight to his Commanding Officer's praise.

An Unusual Christmas
This letter from Private J. Pearce gives a vivid picture both of the miseries and of the lighter side of life in the trenches.
The incident at Christmas described here was repeated again

and again right up the line. Both sides took a holiday on Christmas Day, even from their hates.

From Private J. Pearce, Royal Fusiliers. June, 1915.
'I think I am the only Tommy (regular soldier) serving out here who is a member of the Working Men's College. I am sorry to say there are not many of us left now, although the regular battalions are still maintained. . . . I have served five months in the trenches. . . . During the winter life in the trenches was terrible, it was common to have to wade through water up to the knees. We almost worked day and night to clear the trenches of water and mud . . . sometimes we had to dig another trench which was dangerous work . . . another great trouble at that time was that the earth being sodden with rain the sides of the trenches and dug-outs used to fall in, depriving us of a lay down for several nights. . . . The German trenches were not far off from our line and occasionally they would have a concert which usually ended with them shouting across to us such sayings as: "Fix bayonets." "We are coming after you." "You will never see London again." "Are we downhearted!" to which our fellows shouted back a suitable (but unprintable?) reply.

'Christmas was the most peculiar time as occurred in any war. The German troops came out and met our fellows halfway between the trench lines, where souvenirs, principally composed of buttons and badges, were exchanged, also addresses were given of Germans who had come from London so that we could visit them after the war. During the time I was in the trenches, with the exception of Christmas, sniping was carried on day and night by the enemy . . . consequently almost every day some of the regiment were placed on the famous Roll of Honour. . . . During March I was marked down as temporarily unfit for duty in the trenches, so I was given a billet in the ammunition convoy train . . . to take charge of the ammunition train . . . for the advanced ammunition bases which are near the firing line. . . . It is not a bad job . . . we travel to different places and get a good idea of the general conclusion of things out here.'

XII

MORE LETTERS FROM B.E.F., FRANCE

FROM Rifleman Shaw, 1917. (Later killed in action.)

This first letter from Shaw is a fragment, with no clue to whom it is addressed, but it was probably sent to Pocock.

'... Soon a battery of 6-inch guns start in earnest. Sleep is impossible, so you pack up and try to seek consolation at the Y.M.C.A. with a mug of tea, a half franc packet of biscuits ($\frac{1}{4}$ lb) and a six months old *Byestander** ... The out-of-date magazines get on one's nerves; does no one send modern issues to the troops, or does the censor forbid? Where I am now one can get the Paris edition of the *Daily Mail*. ... The June number of the *Journal* was read amid the horrors of Bullycourt. ... I am just off to an estaminet; the *Journal*, two fried eggs, bread and butter and coffee—yes, it will be a "good war" as we say, for the next hour. ... I have enjoyed reading of the dear old College, but the news of the death of Mr Wade came as a shock to me ... he was the intellectual giant of the literature class ... I valued him highest as a friend ... I shall not forget his kindness to me.'

Written on a later date.
'At present I am well behind the lines where there are whole

* An illustrated magazine. Ceased publication soon after the war.

houses and real civilians. You can realize what a welcome change it is to be amongst same when for months we have been amongst nothing but trenches and ruins; many of the villages have nothing standing but the board with their names. To be just you can hardly blame old Fritz for all of the devastation, much must have been done by our guns in ousting him. . . . Sometimes in these villages you find a remnant of a well set out garden . . . rose trees that still persist . . . you are just going to have a rest, when your eye catches sight of a howitzer a few yards away skilfully hidden in another part of the garden . . . you go to sleep . . . the gun is fired . . . you are too used to gunfire to wake . . .'

From another letter, also from Rifleman Shaw and opening: 'Dear Mr Pocock,
'The following incident may make you realize the hatred we get for the Bosche.
'Whilst peering into No Man's Land I saw a wounded Englishman trying to crawl towards our lines. He was about 150 yards away when I saw him. A white bandage round his head was easily discernible (he wore no hat) and there was no mistaking the fact he was badly wounded. I could see him plainly for it was broad daylight. He seemed to lose his sense of direction for he looked round to see his whereabouts. I waved to him. He saw me and started crawling in our direction. He must have struggled from shell hole to shell hole. Both sides must have seen him. Suddenly a shot rang out from just near him and he rolled over dead. I need not tell you how mad with rage I felt that Fritz should snipe a badly wounded man. I mention this incident as it is characteristic of the brutality that the war is being pursued with by the Bosche. If you were out here you would realize that we are fighting cleaner than the Hun, and I think because of this, and because our cause is right, that God will eventually give us that victory we all so earnestly desire . . .
'What happy and profitable evenings we used to have in Mr Pitt's class. . . . May the Reading Circle help to perpetuate his memory and keep alive and strong that splendid College spirit which he infused into all of us who came into contact with him. I feel certain that this splendid College spirit which is the soul of the College, will be strong enough to make the College

weather these rough times, and after this war what a rush of members there should be! No one can resist the call of the College Spirit!'

From the same. November 3rd/17.
'Dear Mr Pocock, I am sorry to see such a long list of names in the casualty list. The College certainly is "doing its bit". My friends here seeing the *Journal* were keenly anxious for more information concerning the College, many expressed a strong desire to join when peace comes once more. Unfortunately many of these are no more, we were cut up terribly on July 1st. If every fighting member of the College took the names and addresses of friends interested – I have found there is a great desire for more study and education – I feel sure the College membership after this war would be greater than ever. And the same spirit would prevail.
'*P.S.* Bob Hagerty is somewhere up the line. He won one prize for reciting and another for singing.'
(Bob Hagerty was famous in the College for his rendering of 'Macnamara's Band' and certain Savoy opera numbers at College entertainments. He died comparatively young between the wars.)

Driver Pegram, Royal Horse Artillery, in a long letter of no special interest ends with a few lines that paint vividly the side of an artilleryman's duties that now, except for State occasions, belong to history. 'I know you will excuse this pencilled letter,' he writes, 'and that you will understand that the inconveniences of camp life and the *grooming of very large and healthy horses* and the work of artillery generally make the pen rather a nuisance to hold.'

The two letters quoted below provide a study in contrasts. The first from a Tommy in the trenches in France, the second from an officer in Italy.

From Pte. Bob Hagerty, London Scottish, B.E.F., May 1917.
'We have been in the thick of it lately, and "went over the top" last week and captured our objective, but were allowed no peace for days, and the men were very glad when the time came

to be relieved, as we were all absolutely fagged out. Our great difficulty was the water question, and as the weather was so hot, it was most distressing to hear us asking when *would* water be coming. We could hardly speak, but with it all the boys stuck to their work and gave Fritz a hot time. On getting into the trench I came upon a splendid machine-gun and soon got our sergeant to find someone to work it, it was not very long before we had it turned on to Fritz. . . . This part of the line is painful to see, with towns and villages absolutely smashed to atoms, hardly a wall standing in some of the places. . . .'

From Lieut. A. E. Homewood, the last 'Lowes Dickinson Scholar elect', July 1917.

From H.Q. British Artillery, Italy. 'So I have got to Italy, but not with the Lowes Dickinson; and my sketching here is to say the least, problematical. I have known Turin as the walls of a railway station; Milan and Verona, Bologna and Padua as names called out in the night; twice I have passed through Florence – asleep! But I have seen Rome! . . . In the course of certain negotiations it seemed to me good to go to the fountain head. I spoke to the fountain head. I spoke to the General and the dear man packed me off forthwith. After a jaunt of eighteen hours or so I stood, tired and filthy as only these trains can make one, in Rome . . .

'I had to put in much of my time in Embassies and Ministries and such dull places, but I did Rome till I was dead-beat and melted, and my feet literally blistered. But I was happy. . . . I got treated as a distinguished stranger – no end of a time. Truly if we ain't got no money, we do see life!

'Then I came back to where things go bang – The work part of the trip, incidentally, was quite a success, and I have been patted on the head; better I have been spontaneously thanked by a Tommy. I live in a villa which in England would doubtless be christened "Mountain View" – all modern conveniences; two bathrooms (not functioning), stabling (used for other purposes), "extensive grounds back and front". These are adorned with all sorts of things from one trench complete with camouflage, to diverse bad statues of classical persons. . . . Fritz Josef dropped us a reminder recently and there is a hole where Prometheus stood, and he sent Pluto to Hell too. Put the wind up us, but I think he gave his gun position away doing it, and they knocked him out.'

From: Sergt. P. Pornell, B.E.F., 28.8.1917.
'We had a couple of German airmen in wounded the other day – machine brought down by our "Archies".* They both landed in a pool, so were in a nice state when we received them. We gave them a warm sponge down, dressed their wounds, supplied hot drinks and dried their clothes – they cried with thankfulness – didn't expect such treatment in English hands – one of them was an officer – what a sight to see a Hun officer weeping, eh?'

From the same, December, 1917.
'I have to thank you for sending from those wonderful College people, the parcel of comforts. Mrs Simmon's Christmas pudding is of course the feature, and "glory be" there is a piece [left for him] although I little expected it! . . . There seems, to judge from the newspaper articles and letters, some little anxiety at home about the Western Front. I believe it is unfounded, but I can assure you that we are getting very anxious out here about the pacifist propaganda and its unchecked progress. What a pity that the speeches of your Principal and General Maurice and others could not be given to audiences of thousands instead of hundreds. Or the *Journal* containing the account of the speech, exchange circulation for once with one of the popular newspapers.'

From H. Neasel, January, 1918.
'My dear Taylor,
'Allow me to thank you for the package of brain food. The papers were very acceptable. . . . I regret not having seen you when I called at the College and your office. . . . My impressions of the general state of England were not pleasant. I have now been back some three weeks (in France) and found my section working under pleasanter conditions than when I left it in June last. The majority of my old comrades have disappeared but that does not account for the change. I find the N.C.O.'s have dropped the Farnborough touch and are getting more in line

* Soldier slang for anti-aircraft gun.

with the infantry type which so far as my experience goes is the best type out here. With return to the R.F.C.* my work has changed and I am now more indoors than out, working on the side which may be termed the intelligence branch of our service. It certainly gives me a greater respect for this service, and also for the infantry if that were possible. We are encamped in a small clearing under Nissen huts surrounded by trenches and wire and all the debris left by the Germans when forced to retire. Every house is battered to the ground although it must have been a pleasant flourishing village. Fritz made it a pretty thorough stronghold. . . . Just behind the camp is the village cemetery, vaults broken open, headstones scattered, the place a thorough wreck. Curious however that the calvary overlooking this graveyard still partially remains, with the figure of Christ still clinging. Nearby . . . about a dozen graves of French and German soldiers have been dug. It strikes one as strange that on one cross he (the German) has written that it is occupied by a French "Kamarad". A visit to the cathedral town nearby shows that it is now being opened up by the returning civilian population. Many shops have stocks of goods, the most enterprising being a picture dealer selling artists colours and requirements. Evidently he anticipated an early peace and being inundated by the tourists and painters . . .'

Here is another letter from Hagerty, jubilant and hopeful, in complete contrast to the mood of the earlier letter written in May 1917.

From R. Hagerty, 1st London Scots, March 1918.

We were supposed to go to Germany but it was altered and we are now in the army reserve. When the news came in it was just after the last battle just outside Mons, and we moved back to a place called Blaregries . . . then on to our present place, Givry, a village due south of Mons, which is now our winter headquarters. It is a big village, the inhabitants are very hospitable, they have not suffered much while Fritz was with them and they seem to be fairly well fed. The absence of fat was their great loss, soap they cannot get. . . . What a treat to look forward to a winter out here without going into the

* Royal Flying Corps.

trenches. No words can tell you what it is like – trench warfare – it was diabolical in every sense of the word during winter months.

'Well, Pocock, I am delighted to hear they have got news of Harold [Pocock's son, posted missing] I have seen some poor lads and it makes you feel very bloodthirsty towards Fritz. By Jove, Fritz would have got it if he had kept it up much longer. Very often we infantry were out of touch with our artillery, our advance being more rapid than anticipated. Thank heaven, it is all over and we can look forward to being home and back at the old College again soon.*

'The parcels will no doubt be very welcome again to the boys. In this village the canteen only gets stuff twice a week – the peasants sell toffee and ice cream sweets at 2d. *each*!!! the same sweets we could buy in a packet for about 4 oz for 2d.'

From Cpl. F. Wright, 19.3.1918.

'The drawback of living in the midst of "somewhere" is the inability to read anything requiring concentration and of writing a letter consisting of more than two words. The *Journal* – what a host of happy College memories it awakens. It is indeed a tonic and an incentive to carry out the words of Mr Britling [hero of H. G. Wells' novel] and "see the thing through".'

The same.

'One is introduced to a new "vocab" full of original phrases. Do you know what "no bon" or "na pooh" is? Can you "make" things, or "blister" to them? Are you a good "scrounger"? Is your job a "cushy" one? What time of day is "pip emma", and what is "umpteen"? Is a "gasper" food or drink? This looks like the beginning of a modern newspaper quiz!'

Second Air Mechanic H. E. Nye. Kite Balloon Section, R.F.C. also writes of things archaic in warfare.

'I witnessed the first of recent advances from a commanding

---

* The advance described took place early in March, with the enemy well on the run. But, as historians will have spotted, the writer of this letter was too optimistic. Later the Germans made a successful counter attack and pushed our troops well back. Though a shock and depressing at the time, it was a short-lived success.

position. . . . On the second day after the initial push my journeyings took me into the German trenches. . . . The ground is far from being cleared up, "dud" shells, grenades and bullets in every direction. . . . Probably we handle the most awkward instrument of war out here. It is particularly noticeable on taking the balloon from one place to another. Your journey may be only a mile as the crow flies, but the change may involve about ten miles over fields, up and down trenches, under wire, across railways and streams, etc., etc., each man dangling at the end of a rope. We look like a gang of men taking a white elephant to market. Nobody loves us, and nobody wants us, as we struggle on, trying to find a resting place for our monstrosity, and knowing full well that there is no rest for us until we have put this creature to bed . . . change of camp always means a week's strenuous work, and ballooning as a whole is one continuous round of hard work and broken rest, as a balloon is always in action. Like an infant she has to be continually fed, her bottles are gas tubes weighing $2\frac{1}{2}$ cwt. each. . . .'

H. E. Nye, November 1918.

'We came out of the line about three weeks ago for a rest which we had at Helemes near Bemain. The inhabitants left behind made us pretty welcome as far as their circumstances would permit. We are now at Arques near St Omer, making up for our brief rest. I cannot say we are a particularly happy crush, rather preferring being up the line than down here at the base. A fair number of Jerry prisoners are engaged here, but it constitutes a convalescent home for them, as our hours are longer than these prisoner's, our only advantage being that we are at liberty to go out sometimes in the evenings. Such is our reward. We are helping meanwhile in the clearing up, not particularly strenuous work, merely the conditions and primitive methods that prevail have a tendency to make it harder. As regards the past, after going through Drocourt-Queant line, resting a night in Cambrai where we were the first balloon in there, we eventually arrived at Verchain . . . about 800 yards short of Valenciennes. . . . On my return I passed through Douai which has not been so badly damaged as might have been anticipated. Bethune was on a par with Arras; the outskirts of Lens showed a barren wilderness of brick and rubble. . . .

MORE LETTERS FROM THE B.E.F., FRANCE

Refugees who had been deported to other villages and who had managed to escape before the Germans arrived were all making tracks for their homes, the majority with what they could carry on their backs, whilst others had managed to scrounge a cart which they pushed before them. Before leaving Helemes there was great excitement at the arrival of a couple of oxen, a rarity in these parts as Jerry denuded the country of all stock and cattle. . . . After seeing all the ruin and the country laid waste one feels that Germany has got off lightly. One can only hope that the remainder of the peace terms will make them feel the discomforts of this war for many years to come and bring it home to the individual enemy subject. One would have been glad to see their land laid waste and the inhabitants fleeing for their lives. So far the terms bring no real punishment only confiscating and a humbling of their pride, but good enough to go on with.'

From Corpl. B. April 1919. Army of the Rhine.
'Had I not been anticipating demobilization your letter re. keeping in touch would not have been necessary. . . . At present I am on the Rhine a few miles away from Cologne. I must say the people are quite affable but whether through fear I cannot yet judge. The shortage of food without doubt was the beginning of the end. I am billeted in the house of a former machine-gunner who was in the great German push at Cambrai 1918. He tells me that for months the higher command had repeatedly declared England to be starving, that in London alone four or five hundred people a day died of starvation and that in the next month England would be forced to give in. This the soldiers believed until they fell upon well-stocked Expeditionary Force Canteens and had the time, as well as the shock of their lives. It opened their eyes – for an E.F.C. to a half-starved soldier is a sight for the Gods – and they "kicked". Their people at home soon got to know and this in itself helped to hasten the end. We used to wonder where Germany got her soldiers from. This same chap was on four different fronts (including Palestine) during six months.'

XIII

LETTERS FROM MANY THEATRES OF WAR—EUROPE TO THE FAR EAST

THESE letters are not in chronological order, but have been arranged in groups according to the theatre of war from which they were sent, as this, rather than the actual date of writing, seems to make a more coherent story.

From time to time Gibraltar becomes 'news'. Thus these extracts of letters from Gibraltar in 1916 have a certain intrinsic interest.

Gibraltar
From Private Keating (late of the Chemistry class).
'I have been on the "Rock" for ten weeks now . . . one meets all nationalities . . . the men wear many coloured clothes, but the women all wear black as if in mourning. The lower class natives live on food such as is usually given to pigs. The leavings from the soldier's meals are put into huge barrels and the people pay a penny a dip and chance what they get. Fruit is very cheap, but has to be washed before eating as there is a good deal of colic about. It is nothing to have 48 hours rain right off the reel.'

From Sgt. Jennings, *en route* for India.
'. . . Our ship is a good sailor, but her steam steering-gear broke down in the Bay of Biscay. This was repaired at Gibraltar,

but delayed us for nearly six days. During these days our troops marched ashore twice as battalions, with bands playing. We marched through Gibraltar – harbour and town to the Spanish frontier – or rather, the neutral strip. This strip of land has one road running through it which leads from Gibraltar to Spain. Spanish and British troops must not cross this road at the spot where the road leaves the neutral ground, and becomes Gibraltar. This spot is just an opening less than twenty feet wide, in a high iron railing, and is guarded always day and night by Spanish and British sentries, who face each other. It was strange to see for the first time a British sentry *at attention* with his back to troops marching past.'

From Lieutenant A. E. Homewood, January 1918, Italy.
'Dear Pocock,
'I ain't in France, not by many kilometres. I'm in a little corner of Italy, immersed in snow and mountains, and slush and railway trucks and work.... Gad! I'm so tired. I have to start my official correspondence about midnight, and my personal letters when I've done.... I've just got a bundle of reading matter from the College, for which many thanks. This month's *Journal* not to hand yet, but I still hope.... The plucky tone of the *Journal* is a real tonic, and I'm glad to see the college spirit is undimmed.

'But to what a college shall we return! The news about Bailey hit me harder than I can say ... I had been dreading it, fearing it with a sort of premonition. So many of our best had gone. How could one hope that the best of all could be spared.... We wrote one another letters while I was in Egypt. Now he will write no more. Would to God I could have died for some of these better men. I am tired out. Good night.'

Written from Cyprus, from Pte Leonard of the Egyptian Expeditionary Force, dated 1917. Base Signal Depot, E.E.F.
'Dear Guv, As a tailor wears the shabbiest clothes, so does the printer use the poorest paper. How have the mighty fallen. This is a sheet torn off a note-pad which is the best I can lay my hands on. We have had some experiences, with the accent on the some.

'First we left Egypt on a Saturday and lost our week-end.

Still, as we receive 4/- for six weeks pay it was just as well. We had cultivated quite a decent thrust but as beer is 10 disasters (piastres) a bottle, it was wasted. We had a good two days at sea, travelled second class (still on what was left of the aforesaid 4/-) and on arrival here motored to camp, guarded by a fierce battalion of Scots. . . . We slept in huts, so did about 10 million bugs, also ants, mice, crickets and beetles. The slaughter was terrible but the bug won. After about six days of this we packed up all our worldly goods . . . and started off in two bullock wagons driven by two native boys with about 12 words of English and four cuss words. They know more of them now. We had to go about a 12 mile journey at the breakneck speed of 2 miles an hour. At first the roads were fair, then rocks appeared then it was all rocks and no road, then the driver got lost; we kept going till just on sunset. The boys wanted to drop us and go back, but we put the bar up, and at last fell in with a boss-eyed brigand who offered to guide us for a consideration. Bang went the last of my four bob!'

Both in manner and in matter Private Leonard's letter bears a remarkable resemblance to the missives sent from Italy and the Middle East by Fred Catt in the Second World War.

'However,' [the letter continues] 'in the light of the merry old moon we scrambled over the blinking rocks to within two miles of our destination. Here it was impossible for carts to get any further, so we took our stuff off and camped in the open for the night. Next morning I had a lovely map of the island [Cyprus] on my face, arms and legs, all the rock hills and mountains beautifully done in mosquito bites. We had breakfast, then managed to get some native to shift our stuff on donkeys. However, here we are, all dressed up, and nowhere to go: "water, water, everywhere, and not a drop to drink". But still merry and bright [a quotation from a popular song of the time]. By the way, the nearest drinking water is three miles away and has to be carried on donkeys. When we walk round we have to hop like goats. It's the goods, Guv: We have built a little fireplace in a little bit of sand and are very hot at the cooking. Porridge for breakfast (cooked in an empty jam tin) stew and boiled rice for dinner (when there are any jam tins – we are *very* lucky, we have finished two tins). Tea and sardines in the evening, also jam at times. I think we shall be relieved every two or three weeks, but we are regular Robinson Crusoes now.'

Unfortunately there seems to be no record of who 'Guv' was, Pte Leonard concludes his letter with regards and messages for a number of students. . . . It seems most likely that the letter might have been addressed to either Pocock, who was very much a 'father figure' in the common-room, or to the Superintendent, Duchesne.

The Palestine Front
From Cpl. Christie, London Regt. M.E.F.*
'We have had quite an exciting time out here, and I am sorry to say I have been wounded in the head by shrapnel . . . but hope to be back again soon and have another go at the Turk. He is a very fine fighter, and much fairer than the German. Our boys are covering themselves with glory, it is fighting all the time and no rest.'

Here is a later letter from an apparently somewhat disillusioned Christie.

September 2nd, 1917.
'I am in hospital suffering from the effects of my old wound – but hope to be out again very soon. I was in both battles at Gaza and was fortunate to get through without a scratch. The whole campaign has been a series of blunders, nearly rivalling Mesopotamia for inefficiency. . . . We have a different general now and it is marvellous for anyone who was under the old command to see how things have been put on a workmanlike footing . . . which let us hope will mean success.'

After the action that won Christie his V.C. his commanding officer, Major Hammond, wrote a charming letter to his mother, from which the following is an extract:

'I am writing to tell you how proud I specially am of L/Cpl Christie . . . it required tremendous courage that night on the

* This letter was written before the action in which Christie won his V.C.

SOLDIER 1939–45
BILL WALDER
*Royal Armoured Regiment
(wounded North Africa)*

SOLDIER 1914–18
CORPORAL CHRISTIE, V.C.
(wounded Palestine campaign)

hill, when the air was full of every possible device for causing death, when the only place with the least possible degree of safety [and there wasn't much even there] was to stick in the trenches, to get out and go alone along the top of an unknown enemy trench in the darkness. . . . Many a decoration has been won by what is known as a "mad minute", but not in this case, for it was a deliberate act, bristling with difficulty, but of the greatest possible value to the battalion, and at that particular time to the whole of a big operation . . .

'It is doubly pleasing to know that everyone thinks he deserved the fine decoration. . . . It is doubly pleasing to me, as I have always maintained that the fellow who has the moral courage to go to a Bible class on Sundays in England, when most young men waste their Sundays hopelessly, will be the truly brave one when the chance comes. . . . I have told him that now everyone in the battalion knows him and therein comes a double responsibility with his influence, and I hope that he will remain modest and simple-minded, and not be spoilt by the fuss which is naturally made of him. I don't think he will . . .'

From Trooper E. R. Gillingham, Palestine, 1918.

'I also thank you for the College *Journal* which I receive although I am afraid many have gone astray as I have been constantly on the move since the offensive started here, what with the very bad weather . . . and long lines of communication over the desert it is rather a heavy task for the mail to reach us. . . . I have been right through the offensive without mishap. I was one of the first to enter Jerusalem with the H.Q. staff after the city fell into our hands and we were given a very flattering reception, especially from the Europeans. . . . I have managed to visit most of the historical places here, and in Bethlehem we are having a well earned rest, getting ready for the next round.'

After the war General Lord Allenby (affectionately and perhaps a little rudely known to his troops as 'the Bull') gave one of the Saturday lectures at the College on the Palestine campaign.

I do not know if it was the writer of the above letter or another College student from the forces in Palestine who, after the lecture in the Maurice Hall was concluded, asked if he could speak to the General. He was duly introduced – 'I was present at the taking of Jerusalem,' he said eagerly, 'I saw Lihman von Saunders escape in his pyjamas.' 'Then,' retorted Allenby, 'why the hell didn't you stop him!' and turned an angry back on the abashed ex-soldier.

1916.

Lieutenant Munro's letter from Gallipoli is comparable in its style and descriptive vigour to the descriptions of Malta convoys sent in by Lieut. Clements, R.N., in 1942–3. The objective coolness, and unselfconscious courage of the writers shine through both accounts, making them memorable.

Lieutenant Clements' letters appear in the second half of this book.

From Gallipoli, February 1916
Second Lieut. J. J. Munro, Signal Co., R.E. Writing on September 23rd from the Australian and New Zealand Headquarters, Anzac, he says:

'The September number of the *Journal* has just reached me, and is very welcome. News from England is rare and belated, and letters seem to have a habit of doing a grand tour before they flutter down here. Two months ago I left home: one letter has arrived. I suppose that the nature of the campaign here is unique, due to the configuration of the land. Sharp and precipitous headlands, gleaming yellow in the brilliant sunshine, jut out into the deep blue sea. Between them sweep the bays with shelving beaches and a meagre area of flat land, while in every case the land sooner or later rises up in steep cliffs, cut in fantastic zigzag fashion by scrub-clad gullies. These twist about inland, surmounted by sharp-backed ridges, the whole gathering itself up into the great heaps known as 971 and Achi Baba. It is difficult country to campaign in, superbly designed for the defensive, and, one might think, if the fact were not already otherwise, impossible to take from the sea. In rare instances a larger plain is interposed between the high headlands. These are, of course, like many parts here, visible to the Turks, and unhealthy places. I had recently to build across such an area, and received some attention from snipers and shrapnel, while our own guns, of larger calibre than the Turks', were busy demolishing a ridge above and beyond us. The roar of the shells over our heads, the explosion and fountain of earth and stones that flew upward, the occasional "ping" of bullets and bursts of shrapnel, made the place fairly lively. From other points of view the plain was interesting; its flora and fauna would have delighted Jim Holloway; the plants were mostly prickly thistles and tough scrub, with blue-green cactus, fig, mulberry and oak. There are thousands of locusts, coloured lizards, occasional butterflies, tortoises, and snakes. Birds are rarer nowadays but there are some pretty ones. The place swarms with great ants, and the flies are prodigious in number. (Two dead men lay on the plain in one spot: some time there apparently.) The country must all have been of this wild nature before the M.E.F. landed here. Now, as far as we have got, roads have been made, dug-outs constructed, stores collected, guns put in position, and trenches and saps cut: incredible labour has been lavished everywhere, and we enjoy a measure of comparative security which, in the circumstances, is remarkable. The Turks shell us with daily doses; their snipers patiently snipe day after day, and men daily get knocked out; and aeroplanes come over and drop bombs; but we all have reason to be grateful for such security as we have, and men are full of optimism. There is the greatest belief in the higher command here: we believe big movements will come at the right time, and nobody doubts their success. In view, too, of what has been accomplished at the landing, the scaling of these apparently inaccessible sea-walls, all this confidence is justified. If *this* could be done, such men could do anything that remains. The Australasians are wonderful soldiers, big and brawny, and splendidly proportioned. Their uniforms are well cut, and superior to those of the British troops. They seem fearless to the point of recklessness. They can also swear.... They charge with irresistible dash and enthusiasm. One might sometimes think the war a game when watching them. It is perhaps a sort of instinct in the British people so to regard this job. I remember that a Scottish gunner, when the last charge for Hill 60 took place, having fired the last shell at the Turkish trenches and hearing the burst of rifle-fire which meant that our men were charging, leapt on a box by his gun and waved his hat in the air, crying out: "They're off! They're off!" and I thought of the start of the Boat Race. It is a strange admixture of humanity that we have here: Sikhs, Gurkas, and many other non-combatant Indians in various capacities; New Zealanders, Maoris, and Australians; Egyptians and Greeks; Britishers and occasional Yankees.... My dug-out faces the open sea and looks towards Imbros and Samothrake. "The Isles of Greece, The Isles of Greece!" – and here they are, a never ending source of pleasure to look upon.... In the straits between, the war vessels take their stations, administering their heavy shells and shaking the whole ground. It is a lesson of what sea power means to us.'

The letter below was written to Flint, then registrar in charge of the College office. Dated November 1917 it is signed with a diminutive only. It was sent from East Africa.

'I was very glad to get your letter... letters do not arrive too frequently out here... anyway, one has still books and study to fall back upon.... A branch of the good old College would do well in the secluded bush, especially for the more frivolous who hear all too frequently the siren call of the outer world. Here the only distraction would be the rather dreary Y.M.C.A., and the gilded truant would be only too glad to seek again the parental bosom and stay there.... Well, my dear friend, the rains have arrived – that is the precursing showers. We here are snug and happy enough – so we ought to stick it if necessary. Perhaps it won't be necessary, for the remaining Bosches out here are undoubtedly getting H— knocked into them now, and the fever bug which bites us all once, will bite them twice, for they are the weaker foe.

'How is the hostel scheme progressing? I enclose P.O. 8/- on the off-chance; if not required in this connection will you kindly dispose of it in your pet fund – the best father must number a pet amid so abundant progeny. Will you also thank the Marks Fellowship for the parcel of papers and *Journals* ... it was quite a treat to see the old "Westminster" (defunct now for many years, then a major evening paper) and besides it conjured up peaceful visions of panelled walls and leather settees and welsh rarebit, shades of the past, in fact! What a wonderful reunion afterwards! I suppose then we shall have to marry and settle down ... and come twice a week to the college (plus special nights, of course).... Can we not tack on an annexe somehow in which to entertain the women, then they will allow us to come every night!'

The writer was in advance of his time regarding the facilities for ladies in the college! The hostel scheme (for W.M.C. students) he refers to was for long a cherished dream in the College. Largely the brain child of Alexander Hepburn, it caught men's imagination and quite a sum of money was collected, one of the contributors being Charles Wright. However, in the years following the war it gradually became clear that the demand for such a hostel simply did not exist. But a small fund had been accumulated, and was augmented, till it became possible to pull down the two houses adjacent to the College, which were in fact College property, and as well as using the site to improve and add to College amenities in many directions, the modern Ellis Franklin Laboratory was built. The hostel fund substantially helped, but could not wholly finance this enterprise.

Lieut. F. W. Finn, Calcutta Battery, R.F.A., writes from East Africa:
'I am delighted to hear that the College men are doing so much for their country. I wish a College company could have been formed and attached to some unit, but whatever the method followed I feel sure that the influence of the men the College possesses will make itself felt wherever they go and in whatever sphere they may find themselves. Dearly as I love the College, I would prefer to have its educational work come to a standstill for the period of the war, rather than that its members should hold back from serving their country in some way or other. I am glad to know that Sir Charles Lucas is back again safely [from Australia]. The College could not afford to lose him at such a time as the present. I have had a very anxious three months. I have a splendid set of fellows who would go anywhere and do anything. Throughout my life I have never felt my responsibility as I do now. We are in a district abounding in game of all descriptions, lions, leopards, hyenas, wild pig, wart hog, different kinds of gazelle, rhinoceros, giraffes, and very many varieties of deer. We shoot all our meat, make our

own bread, and generally depend on our own initiative for existence. We are all fit and well, and although the prospects for Christmas are not of the brightest, we shall make the best of them. We haven't any gold lace, but I'm certain you would be pleased to see us hard at it in shirts and shorts. To be on guard on a dark night, with lions and other wild beasts howling around, is excellent training, and we are all quite used to it by this time. I will send you my usual donation to the College and *Journal* sub. as soon as I get the opportunity. Please remember me to all at the College.'

L/Cpl T. W. Chapman writes in 1918:
'I spent . . . nearly three years in India. . . . At present I am in the desert sighing for India, with all its imperfections. Mesopotamia is a horrible country to live in, though it is wonderful in many ways. Thanks for your kind wishes . . . may success attend the work of the Marks Fellowship. It is a wonderful work, and we absent members appreciate it.'

News of Prisoners of War in the First World War
News from college men who were prisoners of war was sparse, their numbers apparently few. From these letters it would seem that in some respects their lot was even harder than that of their fellows in the second war. Letter writing also appears to have been more restricted. That is the impression gained from the available correspondence. It does not follow that a wider experience would confirm it.

Note from the Journal, 1918
'Of the College men who are prisoners of war little has been heard. One was placed on the parcel list of the R.A.M.C. Prisoner-of-War Fund. Bread is sent to him . . . every week through Denmark, sixteen parcels monthly. We have not heard however, whether he has received these parcels of bread.'

Rifleman G, captured March 23rd, 1918, sends his 'Thanks for bread – ten loaves received'. They took ten weeks to reach him and arrived mouldy, but he 'managed to use them'.

Another P.O.W. writes 'the sentry is fond of clubbing people, so you see life is a little uncertain'.

LETTERS FROM EUROPE AND THE FAR EAST

An officer stationed in Egypt writes 'there is no doubt we [the British] are the nation who gives prisoners a really good time. Johnny Turk was never better off in any generation since the Flood.'

It is perhaps relevant to recall here that among the letters written during the Second World War, one written from France in 1944 grumbles that the prisoners working from a near-by prisoner-of-war camp are getting lighter working hours than men in the British Army at the same place, employed on similar fatigues!

XIV

THE END OF AN ERA

THE end of the Great War of 1914, the war that was to 'end wars', came at last with the signing of the Armistice in France on the eleventh day of the eleventh month in 1918.

Many sore trials lay ahead, but of these, the men and women, released from the agonizing tensions of war, were mercifully ignorant.

A great wave of relief and thankfulness surged over the country.

The College expressed this feeling in its own fashion, which was after the way of its Principal, Sir Charles Lucas.

His message to the men on their return from the fighting services is typical of the era that was brought to a close by the end of the war.

The spirit that burned in his words survives, but in more muted form. Possibly because in a world torn and disillusioned by two great wars, confidence is shaken, and the flame cannot burn so clear.

The years that separate us from these events today, in the 1960's, are too few. We live still in their shadow, and to that extent our vision inevitably is dimmed.

Welcome Back! April 1919

The Common-Room Committee and its secretary, Dimes, arranged a splendid gathering in the common- and coffee-rooms on April 26th to welcome back to the College the first hundred or so of the men who had been in the forces and were 'demobilized . . . about 240 (hosts who had not been in the Forces and guests who had) were present altogether. The first toast was proposed by Mr Lupton . . . 'to the glorious and immortal memory of those of our fellow members who have laid down their lives for their country in the war'.

This toast was solemnly honoured.

'The Marks Fellowship is giving to each man who has served abroad a fountain-pen . . . each received with his pen a letter from the Principal welcoming him back, and conveying in words such as Sir Charles Lucas chooses so well, our gratitude for those who had done their duty across the sea. Musical honours were then heartily given for the men back from Overseas.'

J. A. Christie, V.C., greeted with cheers, returned thanks on behalf of the guests for the kind welcome they had received.

Songs and choruses were sung, then 'Lieut. Dell rose to address us, and eulogized the minority left to carry on the College work during the war. . . .'

In December 1918 Lucas addressed to every College man who had served or was serving in the Forces a letter 'enclosing a copy of a resolution which was unanimously passed by the Council of the College, and of the few words with which I moved it.'

'We thank you heartily,' the letter began, 'for what you have done to uphold the honour of our College and of our nation. . . . In the name of the college, proud of and grateful to its sons, I wish you with a full heart the happiest Christmas.'

The Resolution

'At their first meeting after the conclusion of the Armistice, the Council wish with all reverence to place on record their thankfulness that the war has been carried to a successful issue; to recall with sorrow, but with pride, the memory of the College men who have fallen in the war; and to assure those who have been spared to come back to us, that we rejoice that they have so worthily embodied the College spirit and upheld the College name.'

The mover spoke emotionally of the war, of our forces, and of his 'loathing for the wickedness that engineered the war'.

THE END OF AN ERA

'Never,' he said, 'did England send nobler armies into the field; never did armies so faithfully reflect all that is best and highest in the English character. Of our College men I would speak in the words of a New Zealand mother, who, in answer to a letter on a wounded son, wrote "I thank God that he has given me men for sons."'

In spite of this highly emotional approach the speech characteristically ends on a down-to-earth realistic note. 'Finally,' Sir Charles declares, 'what has taken place seems to me a call to face the difficult problems which are coming upon us in the spirit of brotherhood that has ever been the spirit of the College, and which has been nobly illustrated in the war.'

Conditions in the College, 1919

The end of the war found the College with depleted numbers, certainly, but otherwise intact; except for the loss of the Maurice Hall, which had been requisitioned as a recruiting station at the outbreak of war, and was not released to the College until 1919. But the clubs were still active and classes both in the humanities and other subjects had sufficient numbers to make them worth running, though the average age of the students attending was inevitably higher than in normal times. It was a condition of affairs that led to a strange distortion.

Though much discussion and consideration had been given in the war years to the future of the College, its emergence as a seemingly flourishing institution at the end of hostilities, left those in power with the notion that their first duty was at all costs to carry on in all the old ways. They failed to recognize that to meet the challenge of the post-war era new methods would have to be devised.

The college needed to be given a new look. Its teaching in many subjects – the art classes were a striking example – had to be modernized if it was to hold its position in the world of 1919 and after.

The inability to appreciate this important problem was to lie at the root of some difficult tussles in the early post-war years, and the brunt of this struggle was to fall upon the resolute shoulders of Ellis Franklin, the Vice-Principal elected in 1921, who held office from January 1922 till 1929.

PART II

The College and World War II
1939—1945

ELLIS FRANKLIN
by Vera Deacon

At her own wish, Vera Deacon has written this tribute to Ellis Franklin.

I am proud to use it as the opening to the second half of this book.

'Those who take an interest in the administration and economics of the Working Men's College, will surely know that Ellis Franklin did indeed "labour for its good".

'He it was who, when he saw the College was in danger of losing its individuality, and becoming one more unit in the London County Council's system of evening classes, took upon himself the task of recouping the Corporation's finances. By investment, by economy and by a well-judged appeal, he made the College free to offer what the Founders intended, a liberal education within the means of the working man.

'For the Clubs, his purchase of the land at Canon's Park, and its development into the beautiful Playing Field, was a service that well deserves that his name should have been given to it in his memory.'

XV

INTRODUCTION

IN 1938, at the request of the Marks Fellowship, I visited a certain woman in Camden Town whose husband, a College student, had got himself a prison sentence through some foolish political activity. In the course of our talk she described to me her recent terror, when a formation of aeroplanes had passed overhead. She had made sure, she said, 'it was the Germans'. Such was the mentality engendered by government leadership in the days of 'appeasement' before the outbreak of war. The Germans it was implied, were too strong for us; it was certain London would be destroyed from the air.

The legitimate horror of war had been translated by oblique propaganda into fear of a potentially aggressive and stronger Germany.

It is necessary to understand these things, and to appreciate the difference in climate between the two great war periods, in order to realize the position of the College in those times. In 1914 the call to arms sounded a clarion note that appealed with irresistible force to the romance and sense of chivalry latent in most men's hearts. The act of rescuing, or trying to rescue, a weak and deluded little nation from the treacherous jaws of the attacking beast, bred a shining enthusiasm that a disillusioned later generation could not emulate.

The peace so shamefully bought at Munich in 1938 was welcomed as a victory of common sense, by a nation cruelly deceived as to the true issues. The outbreak of war tore aside the

INTRODUCTION

veil of pretence, and was grimly accepted. For a year the threat had hung over the nation. The culmination brought something like relief – the tension broke. But no dramatic rescue attempt was even in sight. Poland had been engulfed, Czechoslovakia dismembered piece-meal, while we had helplessly looked on. Instead of the inspiring rescue operation of 1914, when the small band of 'Old Contemptibles' had stayed the German advance at Mons and saved France from immediate defeat, for a year we found ourselves waging what came to be known as the 'phoney war'; the opposing sides facing each other in entrenched inaction, living in holes under the ground like rabbits in a warren. The dreary arrogance of one of the first popular war songs of the day 'Hang out your washing on the Siegfried Line'* well symbolized the spirit of those early months, till Germany, crouching like a beast of prey, sprang suddenly to the attack. The blitz on London, the rape of Holland and Belgium – it was the old savage Germany of 1914.

The débâcle in Norway brought about a change of government, but disaster failed to quell us. Superbly led by Churchill, the country roused from its lethargy. Gone was the complacent bravado of the 'phoney war'. Faced by what outsiders made sure was inevitable defeat, our cities bombed, invasion threatened on our shores, we woke up. Knowing our danger, we kept our courage. Churchill's bleak, magnificent promise, 'All I can offer you is blood, and sweat and tears' roused the nation. We had come to our senses at last.

Within the Working Men's College, from the beginning of the war, a sturdy practical commonsense attitude had prevailed.

The dead hand of officialdom had neither stifled its courage nor paralysed the power for action within its walls. Strong leadership faced up to the problems. Pre-war commitments were largely discarded, a new organization to deal with the changed circumstances was brought into being, and the life of the place continued, different but still strong. This was 1939 – war! and the College had taken on a new look. Here is a quotation from a letter Ellis Franklin wrote to his son at school: 'Yesterday we all went to the College to build a sandbag wall, and paint the windows black. I built a beautiful sandbag wall... if it has not fallen down by Christmas, I will show it to you.'

* The name by which the German entrenched position was known.

INTRODUCTION

The College was certainly transformed, but still a hive of activity. Within its walls Home Guard, Civil Defence workers, and soldiers in uniform rubbed shoulders with the ladies of the Women's Voluntary Services (W.V.S.) and Mr and Mrs Pont, the college caretakers, found their responsibilities strangely changed and multiplied.

Common-room facilities were uninterruptedly maintained, and were a vital point in keeping the corporate life of the place in being.

An attenuated programme of classes that was later increased and varied as demand arose, was arranged for the handful of students that remained, mostly elderly men in the civil service, or on other home jobs.

Bill Barnet, the old stalwart of the College, undertook the manifold burdens of the office, later assisted by Sam Pearse; and from 1942, when Dudley Gill became Superintendent, as it was then called, his neat notices, with their informative rash of little coloured tabs, so familiar to College men of the war period and later, began to appear in his office and in the passages.

In the autumn of 1939 the 'noble rush to the colours' had a different impetus and quality from that of 1914. Many men, both civilian and military, had been called up in a pre-arranged order at the threat of danger early in the summer. Only certain categories of occupation or study, regarded as essential for the national well-being, were exempt from civil direction, or the call to service in the armed forces.

In spite of all this there were large numbers of men reluctant to wait till their turn came to be called, who flocked to volunteer for service with the Navy, Army, or Air Force, in the earliest days of the war.

The College produced its share of such volunteers, many of them still familiar faces in the common-room more than twenty years after the close of the war.

Three of them, Dick Ramage, Geoff Brown and Bill Walder, had managed to join the 8th Armoured Brigade together. Nicknamed by their friends in the College 'the Three Musketeers' they were able to remain together until first Ramage, then Walder, was seriously wounded in North Africa. Walder and Ramage were sent back to England with the first batch of wounded to arrive from that theatre of war. Walder's

INTRODUCTION

picture appeared in a newspaper photograph of the hospital ship as she docked at a British port in January 1943.

Freddie Catt, posted to the Army Pay Corps, spent most of his war service in Italy and the Middle East. His work with the pay-rolls gave him access to information not generally available. He used this unique opportunity in the best possible way for the benefit of the College, taking infinite pains to trace men with whom contact had been lost.

It is a strange thought that, with rare exceptions, the names of the fallen, carved on the oak boards of the Roll of Honour that hang in the entrance hall of the College, will be more familiar to future generations of College men than those of many of the survivors of both world wars, that in their time were 'household words' to their contemporaries.

After all, who in the post-war years remembers the cabinet maker Pegram, old student of the College, who fashioned the board? Or Dark, the wood carver, soft spoken, tall and handsome, student and member of the Dramatic Society, who carved upon it the names of those who fell in the Great War of 1914–18?

XVI

EXTRACTS FROM THE JOURNAL IN THE EARLY DAYS OF THE WAR

THESE notes and reports selected from issues of the *Journal* from 1939 onward, give a picture, fragmentary, but authentic, of events in the College before and after the declaration of war on Germany in 1939.

May–June, 1939

COLLEGE NOTES

'Ellis Franklin, the Bursar, after something like a six months' task in connection with the refugee problem, has managed to take a well-earned rest. All College men are specially pleased that he is back again.'

It is in this connection worth noting that in 1938–9 the College held English language classes for refugees, giving to these sad students, all the privileges of full membership of the College.

A year later a more august journal takes up the tale.

From *The Times*, August 9th, 1940: 'Everywhere language classes are being held for refugees. Good work in this direction is being done by the Working Men's College, Crowndale Road, where Englishmen learning French, and Frenchmen learning English, are proving mutually helpful. Only the other day the two sets were found having coffee together during the break for the (radio) nine o'clock news bulletin.'

EXTRACTS FROM THE JOURNAL 1939-41

By the early summer of 1939 war clouds were already discernible on the horizon. But with stubborn courage and optimism the College prepared for the new session, and persisted in its efforts to raise money on behalf of the Building Fund, that was to be the foundation of a permanent income for the maintenance and improvement of the College premises.

With the end of the session approaching students are exhorted, through the *Journal*, to 'hand in names and addresses to the office as well as particulars, of friends who are likely to come along next session and/or would like to have the programme of classes for 1939 to 1940.'

There follows on this a request to 'students who are, or wish to become annual subscribers to the Building Fund, of five shillings a year, to please pay their subscriptions in at the office...' A continuation of this note reports that 'A. and G. F. Hitchen, brothers, have submitted a suggestion that boxes be provided for odd coppers (or slightly larger sums) to be dropped in, for support of the Building Fund and the Marks Fellowship.' The *Journal* then proceeds to explain an accepted improvement on this plan. 'Such money may be placed in an envelope and dropped into the letter box at the College Office. This (qualified) acceptance of the (Hitchen brothers') suggestion obviates the task involved in making provision for the safe custody of odd removable boxes.'

The Military Training Bill

The call-up in that dangerous summer was put into action before war was declared. A special bill, the 'Military Training Bill', was passed by Parliament for that purpose.

The College *Journal*, under the heading 'Military Training Bill', gives the information that... 'Students of the College called up under the provisions of the Military Training Bill which operates from July 15, 1939, will be entitled to continue membership, including admission to the Common Rooms, for the period of one year, for the sum of 5s. only. A Membership Ticket, formerly Old Students' Ticket, will also be available for those who have attended College classes for four years with a minimum attendance of two-thirds in each class, price 5s.

Another note in the same number of the *Journal* informs its

EXTRACTS FROM THE JOURNAL 1939-41

readers that 'The Harrow U.D.C. are desirous of taking over the Pavilion at the W.M.C. Playing Fields, Edgware, in the event of hostilities.'

The summer of 1939 was consistently fine and warm. It is curious that both in 1914, the year of the outbreak of the first Great War, and in 1939, there was a serenely beautiful summer.

The annual Garden Party and Sports in 1939 was held in June in memorably perfect weather. There was a good programme of sporting events including the time honoured tug-of-war. The Mayor of St Pancras graced the function with his presence, and there was a record attendance of guests.

The *Journal* sums it all up with the remark, 'Most fittingly, the summer session that ended a successful College year, with plans for the next session well matured, closed in sunshine, with a Sports Day and Garden Party, the most successful of any since the new Playing Field had been in use . . .'

Except for a function run jointly with the A.R.P.* in 1940 (who were by then in occupation of the pavilion) this was to be the last College garden party for six years.

Another 'best ever' of that golden summer was the Holiday Club's choice of Nice for their summer quarters. This trip was considered an outstanding success.

Planning for the new session was doggedly continued as the following announcements in the summer number of the *Journal* show . . .

Under the heading 'Important Dates' the College is reminded that 'Founders' Day will be celebrated on Saturday, October 21st, when the Right Honourable Herbert Morrison will speak and present the prizes'. 'The Old Students' Club Supper will be on Saturday, 16th December . . .'

There is yet another hopeful reminder:

'Session 1939–40. Enrolment for the next session will begin on 15th September . . .' The paragraph then discusses the classes planned, with particular reference to new classes in the 'History of Architecture', a class in General Science, an additional law class, and 'the fencing which started in January and has proved so successful that it is being continued'.

Sadly 'wishful thinking' most of this, as later notes in the *Journal* show.

*Air Raid Precautions unit.

EXTRACTS FROM THE JOURNAL 1939-41

There was no Founders' Night celebration in October 1939. The country was at war.

The College doors were still open to students, but its activities, both educational and social, were of necessity curtailed for the period of hostilities.

The notes that follow, quoted from the relevant numbers of the *Journal*, give the story. . . . They are inevitably somewhat scrappy, but they do make up a picture – perhaps rather an impressionist picture – of life at the College in the early phases of the war.

THE FIRST TERM OF THE WAR

College Notes from the Journal, *February, 1940*

A Lighted Sign at the College

'The requirements everywhere to prevent interior lighting being seen in the streets, made it necessary to paint College windows black.' With unexpected results, for it was so effectively done that one student wrote: 'Everything seemed to be shut up.'

However, subsequently the lighting restrictions were slightly modified, enabling the Executive to 'approve the idea of a lighted sign . . . to prevent a recurrence of similar errors'.

There was another lighting problem. As the March 1940 *Journal* explains: 'The common-room with ten windows completely blacked had made it impossible to see into it, or out of it, even, during day-time.' The problem, however, was solved. 'Now blinds are fitted and the black removed so that rays of sunshine may penetrate, until dusk draws on.'

Good Class Attendances. 'With a percentage of class attendance reaching 79·7 per cent, the College may congratulate itself on the fact that classes have been maintained in so many subjects during the term September–December 1939. The language classes both in French and German have enrolled a good number of students, also with a high percentage of attendances.'

An Informal Wartime French Class

'French as she is run' is the heading of a paragraph in the *Journal* in 1940. 'The success of the French class run by the Superintendent (C. Chapman) has been one of the pleasant features of the College during a session that bristles with

EXTRACTS FROM THE JOURNAL 1939-41

difficulties . . . call-ups, blackout, evacuation, rate of sickness, which became the highest for 10 years. The class meets round a nice fire in the Superintendent's room – not an unpleasant inducement to attend during the cold weather which has been experienced. This class also has the advantage of gramophone records used, and the guidance of an enthusiastic and popular teacher.'

A welcome domestic announcement in the autumn of 1939 informs members that 'the College is open from 5.30 p.m. to 10 p.m. each week-night and on Saturdays and Sundays from 2 p.m. to 10 p.m. The usual excellent cooking service is available on Mondays to Fridays inclusive, at lowest possible prices. The age limit for new students has been reduced from 17 to 16 years.'

Social Events

Social events also appear to have prospered at this period; 'The College Orchestra (under Charles Hambourg) has given two concerts, dances have been held regularly, and smoking concerts have been arranged. The Common-Room Committee continues to give the College invaluable help in many ways, and their energetic and willing co-operation has greatly lightened the work of your House Committee.

'It has been particularly encouraging to see members of the College who are on leave at social functions.'

'It takes war,' remarks the *Journal* on another page 'to make the Musical Society play the National Anthem – but they did it at their concert in aid of the Welfare Fund. There was a good attendance . . . in spite of blackout. . . . Charles Hambourg and Freddie Barrett shared the conducting . . . it is good in these times when so many societies are closing down for want of support, to find the Musical Society in going order.'

Charles Hambourg, the Director of Music in the College, was one of the Bursar's importations. A colourful character, genial and forceful, popular and full of enthusiasm, he was the brother of the famous pianist Mark Hambourg, and he succeeded in building up the College music to a standard it has rarely achieved.

The Bursar always liked to maintain that he was not musical. But besides introducing Charles Hambourg to the College, it was he who later insisted that the new building should have, not only laboratories that were up to date, but sound-proofed practising rooms and a rehearsal room for the orchestra.

At the beginning of the war the Old Students' Club meetings lapsed sadly. In 1941 the Club only held one meeting; this was however remedied later, as this brief note in the *Journal* shows:

'The Old Students' Club had eight meetings during the year.'

Administrative Staff. 'In 1943,' the *Journal* states, 'the registrar, W. H. Barnett, who first came to the College in 1886 at the age of 24, retired on pension from its service. He was appointed temporary secretary in 1898, Custodian from 1899 to 1902 and then became registrar. . . . E. G. Pearse (Sammy) has been appointed as clerk in charge of the office under the Superintendent's direction.'

One must elaborate on that bare statement, for the kindness, resource, and helpfulness of these two, especially in relation to the labours of the Work Party, is something that will not readily be forgotten. One could badger them for anything – wrappings for parcels or information, at any hour they would go loaded with packages to the post office – whatever one asked was always readily forthcoming.

XVII

THE COLLEGE AT WAR

Evacuee Ship, A Personal Tragedy
ALMOST at the onset of the war its tragedy, in the starkest form, fell upon a member of the College . . . H. H. Crawley.

There was a movement, sponsored by the government, yet in retrospect seeming to border upon panic, to get children out of the country to what was deemed a safer refuge. Ships were chartered under an approved scheme, most of them bound for Canada or the U.S.A. Crawley decided it would be prudent to part from his two small daughters under this scheme. It was to prove a disastrous decision. In the *Journal*, under the heading 'Torpedoed Evacuee Ship', is this grim paragraph, 'For us all,' the news item reads, 'the saddest note of the war is to record the deaths of Pauline Mary, aged 11, and Shiela Anne aged 9, children of H. H. Crawley. The children left a west-bound port in September in a passenger ship chartered mainly for children . . .' In a tragic communiqué the Dominions Overseas Secretary takes up the tale. Expressing 'horror and indignation that any German submarine captain could be found to torpedo a ship 600 miles from land in tempestuous seas', the statement concludes: 'The conditions were such, there was little chance for passengers, either adult or children, to survive . . .'

The immediate effects of the impact of war on the College itself can best be described in the words of the 'College Notes' appearing in the contemporary numbers of the *Journal*.

1939. War and the College

'The session 1938–9 was successful, particularly when the many difficulties confronting the College during this year are considered. . . . Many teachers and students were actively engaged in various forms of national service. . . .' 'By the end of July all preparations had been made for the forthcoming session, but the outbreak of war in September frustrated all the plans so carefully laid. Fortunately however in the last few days of August part of the College . . . had been blacked out so that it was possible to open without interruption when the emergency lighting regulations came into force. One effect of the outbreak of war was to deprive us at once of the help of many students and teachers, while at the outset the Government ban on evening classes meant that all that could be done was to keep open the coffee-room as a meeting place for members. In these circumstances the Executive at once decided to modify rules . . . so as to permit students in past sessions to take out an old students' ticket without having satisfied all the normal requirements. Accordingly circulars were sent out in September to about 2,500 members and ex-members of the College.' Before the end of the month, however, the *Journal* can report that 'By this time the Government ban on evening classes had been withdrawn, provided there was adequate air-raid shelter for the students in the building. It was therefore decided to proceed with such shelter . . . and attempt to restart classes. . . . Shorthand, Russian, physical training, art and orchestra were offered . . . the first smoking concert took place on October 6th. . . .'

'The reduction of activities,' the *Journal* explains, 'necessitated a reduction of expenditure, and consequently of staff. Generous periods of notice were given to the staff, who, mostly found other work immediately. All have been assured of their places being kept open for them.' The staff that remained, the Superintendent, Cecil Chapman, his assistant, A. J. W. Walker,* Mr and Mrs Pont, the caretakers, and two cleaners were 'admitted to honorary membership of the College during the war'.

As in the First World War, the College proved itself equal to

---

* Owing to the diminished number of students the office of assistant superintendent was abolished during the war. But that did not mean that Walker ceased to assist!

the occasion. 'Thanks to the ready and vigorous help of the Common-Room Committee,' the report continues, 'and the co-operation of the staff, social activities, considering the difficulties, have been well maintained. Dances are held regularly, members of the Common-Room Committee assisting with the serving of refreshments and in other ways, and smoking concerts have been arranged. The orchestra, under Charles Hambourg, has given two concerts. It has been particularly pleasant to see members of the College on leave from war service present on these occasions.'

These activities under war-time conditions are noted as 'encouraging', 'but,' warns the *Journal*, 'it would be foolish to minimize the difficulties that lie in front of us. Every effort is being made to keep in communication with College men in the services' – a matter regarded in both wars as of the utmost importance – 'and the . . . College ladies at the weekly work parties give great help in this direction.'

The Ladies' War Work Party, formed in September 1939 by a group of members' wives with the help of Mrs Ellis Franklin, to knit and sew for College men in the forces, met each week in the secretary's room.

During the First World War a group of ladies had met monthly for a similar purpose at Mrs Lionel Jacob's house, but in 1939 it was felt that the College should be the centre. The scope of the Second World War work party also became a little wider.

The macabre role of mortuary was assigned to the College at the opening of the blitz, and the bodies of the victims of local bombing were duly delivered to the basement. It was in the basement also that as soon as the A.R.P. (Air Raid Precautions) had vacated the premises, the W.V.S. set up their St Pancras headquarters. The old Physics Laboratory was transformed by them into a clothing depot, under Ellis Franklin's wife, a link between the W.V.S. and the College that was to prove vital later, in the days of wool shortage and rationing. Here, in the depot, a motley crowd of Belgian, Maltese and other nationals gathered each day, often waiting in the corridors in long queues that stretched out into the street.

During the early days of the blitz the Maurice Hall housed a clothing store for 'bombed outs' where a crowd of genuine, and not-so-genuine, hardship cases collected waiting hopefully for a free handout of useful clothing. 'Have you been bombed out?' one old man was asked, 'No,' came the frank rejoinder, 'but I heard they were giving out free suits here, so I came along to see what I could get!' On several occasions the local distribution of ration books was made from the College.

In January 1943 the first of the war-time unrestricted Old Students' luncheons – in lieu of a supper, since war conditions made a supper impracticable – was held in the College. Luncheons for a strictly limited number of guests had been arranged by the Old Students' Club and held at the College in 1939 and 1940; in 1941 it was felt that some effort should be made to organize a reunion on a less restricted scale both for the men at home, and for College members who might be on leave from the fighting services. An experimental luncheon was arranged by the Old Students' Club at Lysbeth Hall – in Soho Square – a restaurant that catered for private parties. This function was reasonably successful, but it was realized afterwards that what the men wanted was to meet, not in a restaurant, but in the College itself, that had been part of their nostalgic dreams of home.

Accordingly, the possibility of holding a luncheon for large numbers in the College was investigated, and with the co-operation of the caretakers and the Ladies' War Work Party, it was found that the domestic side could be suitably taken care of, and food for over sixty guests provided legally, without recourse to the precious ration books, except for 'points', that would have to be – and were – hoarded for months for this occasion. ('Points' covered non-essentials such as jam and cheese; basic foodstuffs were dealt with by a meagre system of coupons.)

Geese and turkeys replaced the traditional roast beef, for meat was severely rationed, but birds were 'free' if one could get them! The geese, procured from a farm, arrived in their natural state. As the fishmonger had no labour to pluck them, two of the work party ladies volunteered. Goose feathers grow close and thick, and the creatures had been dead two days. After about three hours' hard labour by the two rash innocents, Roland Franklin, the Bursar's youngest son, on leave from the Navy, and in uniform, arrived unexpectedly on the scene. A fortunate bolt from the blue, gaily he helped the exhausted volunteers through the last phase of their task.

This was to be the first of a series of war-time Christmas luncheons, held in the common- and coffee-rooms. Sixty guests accepted the invitation, eighty came, all were fed. A large proportion of them were men on leave from the services. The meal was organized and served and the food 'scrounged' by the joint efforts of the War Work Party and the caretakers; days beforehand ladies were working in the kitchen trimming sprouts and peeling potatoes. On the morning of the function Ellis Franklin and Mrs Morrison (mother of Ronald, a Vice-Principal of the College between the wars) might also have been seen in the kitchen – she enveloped in a large old-fashioned white linen apron – carving up geese and turkeys for two hours in preparation for the feast. A note in the contemporary *Journal* remarks, the Work Party was 'privileged (on this occasion) to assist Mr and Mrs Pont on the domestic side. They only hope the function in the common-room was as happy as that in the kitchen and serving-room.'

Although in the centre of a network of railways, and thus in a much bombed target area, on only two occasions did the College suffer damage; once from a direct hit, when a number of windows were broken, and the library and part of the roof was damaged, and a glass door in the basement was torn off; and on one subsequent occasion when blast caused some further destruction to windows and doors and the roof of the building.

At night the College gave shelter to many 'strange bedfellows' – ambulance workers and firefighters of Civil Defence, W.V.S. on duty for any emergency that might crop up, and the inevitable bunch of 'D' Company Home Guard and soldiers on various duties, or merely being given refreshments – a sanctuary shared on occasion by an assortment of guests, or even the Franklin dog!

Amid all this present activity and stress, the future of the College remained a topic of lively concern. The advice of experts in particular subjects was sought, always with the aim of keeping up with the most advanced methods of teaching, and obtaining the best guidance available. In November 1943 we find Ellis Franklin writing to his son, 'We had a big Council meeting at Working Men's College to discuss our future. It was an interesting talk. . . . It was considering the report we had been preparing for some months on the future development of the place after the war.' Ellis had experienced the apparent lack of organization and co-ordination of the various groups on the resumption of activities after the First World War.

Reading old documents one is surprised at this. Earnest discussions about the future of the College took place between 1916 and 1918; but these were initiated by a group of elderly men, inspired by a genuine idealism, but working on the assumption, apparently, that a complete return to the *status quo* was the sole aim to try for.

In 1919, when Ellis Franklin joined the College he had felt the place was out of touch with the needs of the new age. Teachers were left to their own devices, and in many instances, methods of teaching long out of date prevailed. Remembering all this, the Bursar and his colleagues were determined that the restoration of peace should find the College not only ready to welcome back old and receive new students, but to offer classes and facilities *in tune with modern needs* that could favourably compare with the highest standards of the pre-war years.

General Conditions in the College

Until the intensive air attacks of 1940 an amazing degree of normal activities continued in the College.

The various clubs and societies continued to hold regular meetings, although one does find a moan from the Chess Club at the difficulties encountered in arranging matches, due to the general dislocation caused by the call-up, and the hours that new civil defence duties added to so many men's working days.

There was a vigorous social life in the common-room, and through the Clubs. The Furnival Cycling Club, egged on by Eric Cooke and other enthusiasts, continued, though with depleted numbers, to ride forth into the country at week-ends.

Every week-day evening, and for one hour on Saturdays the library was open; four nights in the week with Dimes in attendance.

THE COLLEGE AT WAR

Even on Sundays the College was open for a few hours, though canteen facilities were limited to week nights.

Before this was finally decided upon the idea had been considered, and the Superintendent arranged a tea social at which about thirty guests attended, of whom five were ladies. There was afterwards a short discussion about future Sunday arrangements and it was agreed that the College should be open from 3 p.m. till 10 p.m. every Sunday.

Eighteen classes that included languages, mathematics, and shorthand, literature, current events, art, physical training and orchestra, were offered and well attended, at any rate up till March 1940.

There were meetings and discussions by the Old Students' Club, and weekly talks in the Superintendent's room, usually addressed by members of the Executive Committee or the Council, headed by the Principal Sir Wilfrid Greene, and including the Vice-Principal and the Bursar and others.

Feingold* organized a Reading Circle for 'College men who are interested in English literature but are unable to attend the class on Wednesdays with any regularity'. Feingold's circle was to be 'run on quite informal lines . . . the arrangement as to works to be read . . . being made weekly'. Rather oddly, this group, for those 'unable to attend regularly the Wednesday classes', was to meet on Wednesday evenings! Later, when people's working hours became yet more incalculable, and the blitz added its quota to the difficulties of the blackout in the evenings, a few College classes were arranged to take place in the afternoons.

Temporarily, the combined hazards of blitz and blackout reduced College attendances to a pitiably low figure. But as people became more used to 'the terror that flies by night' matters gradually improved, and life in the College revived, though necessarily to a limited degree.

The two serving-room boys, 'Alf' and 'Ernie', having been called up, members of the Common-Room Committee helped with this service.

In 1939–40 the Furnival Treats, the *Journal* observes, were given up 'partly due to the difficulties caused by the absence of street lighting, and the danger that air raids might take place'.

* Feingold was a student teacher.

Rather touchingly, since 'some money had already been received... a sum of one guinea was paid to the Lyulph Stanley School... to make up part of the deficit... in providing treats in the area where the children lived'.

It was remarkable that in 1940 the College could open its doors for seven days in the week, with the complete and cheerful co-operation of its staff.

FRANK GAHAN
Vice-Principal 1937–45

GEORGE BANKES
Teacher. Wartime Chairman of the Playing Field Committee and the Old Students' Club

XVIII

THE COLLEGE AND THE SECOND WORLD WAR. F. GAHAN

THE 3rd September – War! Immediately after the Prime Minister's announcement on the radio, the wail of sirens (albeit a false alarm) brought home to all the knowledge that this time hostilities would involve every man, woman and child in the country.

War was not unexpected. After the false hopes raised by Chamberlain's meeting with Hitler at Munich, there had been a year of intense preparation. The clouds of war became so lowering that urgently to make ready for war was a dominant duty. Readiness might deter Hitler; at the worst it would give resistance a chance of success.

During this year of preparation the work of the College had gone on normally, but many members of the College were committing themselves to war-time activities – joining the armed forces, enrolling as air-raid wardens, or in Civil Defence services; planning how, if war came, they could best help the nation. Older men began to drill with the Local Defence Force – changed with typical Churchillian vigour to the Home Guard – and the civil servants among the teachers and other voluntary workers, found their departments being dispersed far from London. The College was prepared for blackout, and other air-raid precautions were taken.

Enrolment week was held as planned in the second half of

THE COLLEGE AND THE SECOND WORLD WAR

September, but the Executive Committee had decided to reduce the minimum entrance age from 17 to 16, so that the lads who had left school might profit before joining up; this was made known during enrolment week.

Enrolments were down and teachers scarce, but classes continued; the common-room remained open, although the blackout* discouraged the older students from foregathering as had been their wont. The autumn meeting of the Council was held as usual, but instead of the annual Old Students' Supper, a luncheon for about thirty guests was held in the common-room in December.

In 1939 there was no hope, as there had been in 1914, that the war would be over in a few weeks. At the November meeting of the Council in 1939 the main control of the College was put into the hands of an Emergency Committee, composed, in addition to the honorary officers of the College, of men likely to be remaining in London, and able to come to the College as need arose. The College remained open throughout the war, but in September 1940, when the period of heavy nightly air raids began, only nineteen students enrolled, and the common-room was almost deserted.

During the day-time the College building was used by the St Pancras Borough Council and as related elsewhere in these pages, by numerous other bodies, for diverse war-time purposes and activities.

The rents from this day-time occupation of the building, and the unexpended balance of endowments, together brought in a substantial income.

The financial problem, however, was not a mere matter of household accounts.

There remained in the minds of a number of College men a vivid memory of how, as a part of the aftermath of the First World War, the College had been faced with the threatened loss of its independence – having perforce to accept a monetary grant from the London County Council that involved also a degree of control of its classes and fees – and a consequent threat to its most cherished traditions. That crisis stimulated Ellis Franklin, the Vice-Principal at that time, to take steps

* Blackout was enforced outside in the streets as well; no street lamps were lit, shop windows were totally black or dimmed to insignificance.

to raise the money necessary for a substantial permanent endowment fund, that should free the College from the need to accept the Council grant and ensure that the independence thus regained should never again be in jeopardy. He recognized that the danger came not only from the financial straits caused by the war, but also from the lack of funds necessary from time to time to keep abreast of educational development. In due course he became Bursar of the College and Treasurer of the Corporation in 1930 and devoted all his skill, as a successful merchant banker in the City, to improving the College finances. His judgement and skill may be illustrated by his decision to collect the shares of a certain dock company for the College, and his perception of the right moment for disposing of them. For when in 1954 the College celebrated the centenary of its founding, a public appeal for additional endowment funds produced more than £50,000; but the well timed sale of these shares added a clear profit of more than £80,000! So war-time accumulations and wise investment formed the greater part of an endowment fund large enough to provide for all probable demands on the resources of the College for many years.

In 1936, when the College was trying to persuade Sir Wilfrid Greene (later Lord Greene) to become its Principal, he made his first visit to the College while work was in progress on the extension to provide the new Science Laboratories, a gymnasium, music-rooms, an additional common-room and flats for the superintendent and caretakers, at a cost of over £18,000. Sir Wilfrid expressed the hope that this was not what he called 'ecclesiastical finance' – spending on elaborate buildings and equipment in the hope that the money would be raised some time, somehow. His surprise was as great as his satisfaction when told that before any work had been begun almost every penny to pay for it had been accumulated.* He promptly accepted the invitation to become Principal and took great pride in the office, mentioning his holding it in all the books of reference.

The chief fruit of the war years was undoubtedly the thorough reconsideration of the College's educational policy. Great social

* This remarkable achievement was helped by the existence of the 'hostel fund'. A W.M.C. students' hostel being generally regarded as superfluous, the money collected for that scheme formed the nucleus of the fund for this new building.

THE COLLEGE AND THE SECOND WORLD WAR

changes made a startling contrast between conditions in 1854 and 1940. By 1940 there had been seventy years of compulsory education, and in London there were many highly efficient places of adult education. The College was determined to maintain all its peculiar advantages in having a large proportion of voluntary teachers and officers, most of them with University degrees; and in the constant free mixing in the common-rooms and playing field and in the many College societies and activities, of officers, teachers, and students; and of former students who come regularly to the College, frequenting the common-rooms. It could only preserve these unique advantages if the nature and quality of its classes were calculated to attract the young men who would be returning from war service to civil life, or who were growing up in a war-tormented society.

So the Emergency Committee set itself to review with great thoroughness the policy of the College, with a view to ensuring that when peace restored the College to full activity, its members would find its traditions preserved, its opportunities enlarged, and its standing in the world of education enhanced.

The discussions begun in 1942 and continued until 1944.

The Emergency Executive Committee sought and readily obtained the enthusiastic help of many distinguished educationalists, a number of whom continued to come to the College and to give active help when the time came to test the plans after the war. They included (in alphabetical order) Professor E. N. de C. Andrade, F.R.C., Sir Lawrence Bragg, M.C., F.R.S. – whose father had lectured at the College – Canon Adam Fox, D.D., a former professor of poetry at Oxford University, J. C. Maxwell Garnett, C.B.E., Professor J. W. Keeton, Ll.D., Canon Spencer Leeson, then headmaster of Winchester, and Mr Savage, then Education Officer of the London County Council.

This work by the Committee was a wonderful example of co-operative effort. Lord Greene presided over the long series of discussions – the experts enjoyed being intelligently cross-examined – and every proposal and piece of advice was critically scrutinized and tested from every reasonable point of view.

But through all the discussions was the guiding influence of Ellis Franklin, who it was realized was the one person who, from the time when he came to the College in 1919, had given constant thought to the need of a carefully planned policy, continuously applied, if the College was to serve its members and the community as fully as was worthy of its great opportunity.

The ideals and ideas which emerged from the long discussions had to be put into words. There was much drafting and redrafting.

Eventually the Committee was able to put the draft before the Council, where it was fully debated, and after a few revisions here and there, the final draft was enthusiastically adopted.

In 1944, it was published as a pamphlet of twenty closely written pages as 'The Report of Council on the Future of the College'.

When peace came and the College returned to full life, this report bore abundant fruit, and was, as the 'History of the Working Men's College, 1854–1954' truly says, 'a blue print for the development of the College in the post-war era'.

XIX

WAR WORK PARTY

'IT is the aim of the Work Party to render present help in the time of war and still to look to the future and the days of reconstruction.'

(Announcement in the *Journal* on the formation of the Work Party.)

The announcement continues:

'. . . It is believed that . . . when peace returns and the time of reconstruction comes, to have kept together, and kept alive affection and loyal regard for the College, may prove to have some real value in the task of building up, and getting old students and friends back to the College once more . . .'

At its inaugural meeting the objects of the Work Party were defined as:

(1) 'To give the College ladies the opportunity to meet and keep alive the College spirit, looking ahead to the days of reconstruction.'

(2) 'To work for College members and the troops generally.'

(3) 'To maintain a *personal* contact with all students in the forces, that they may the more readily gather together in the College when the days of peace return.'

The Work Party

Announcement in the *Journal*. 'Mrs Franklin has organized a work party of women associated with the College, which is meeting regularly at the College.'

WAR WORK PARTY

The scheme was put up to the Executive Committee who made it a practicable possibility by giving the Work Party a starting grant of £5. (This was in the form of a guarantee that was in fact never called upon.) To launch the scheme, twenty-two College members then known to be in the Forces were sent a circular letter inviting them to use the facilities offered by the Work Party. The highlight of those early days was when a man who had received a pullover asked for eight more 'as there are eight men in this platoon'. One College man asked for socks for each individual in his A.A. Battery. At that time, when the number of College men to be looked after was so small, and official issue for the troops was still inadequate, garments were knitted by the Work Party – always on request – for members to distribute among friends in their units. A parcel sent in response to an urgent request from the B.E.F. was acknowledged with a prompt request for more! Later, owing to the greatly increased number of College men in the Forces, and the difficulties of the wool situation, the practice had to be discontinued, and work sent exclusively to individual College members.

In those early days, work was also undertaken for the British Red Cross, who supplied the materials for all garments made for them; and collections of second-hand clothing were organized for Finland at the time of the Russian attack on that country, and for evacuated London school-children in 1940. After the Dunkirk evacuation a collection of books was made for French soldiers in hospitals in England.

From the first the Work Party received support from the various College clubs. The Common-Room Committee, in place of its usual collection for the Furnivall Treats, opened a fund. The Clubs Association provided money and arranged a dance. The Musical Society raised £6 at a concert.

Though many individual members of the Work Party suffered in the blitz, the meetings continued throughout the war. Often ladies took wool home; after a bad bombing week, one of them would turn up at meetings with up to six completed pairs of socks knitted during raids 'because I like to have something to do'. Another, evacuated to Wales on account of her husband's job, described 'knitting in a cupboard under the stairs' during raids.

Starting with a membership of fourteen ladies the number of

workers had risen by January 30th, 1940, to over forty, many of whom attended College meetings, others worked at home, and a group of Edgware residents affiliated to the Work Party, were organized by the late Mrs H. Macdonald (Elsie).

The Work Party was affiliated to the W.V.S. through the St Pancras Centre that had its offices in the College. It was necessary to acquire this official standing in order to qualify for the supply of wool at wholesale prices for knitting for the Forces, that was allocated only to recognized groups. Later, when the rationing of commodities became general, this recognition became essential to ensure the mere survival of the Work Party.

But as the war dragged on and wool supplies became yet scarcer, the regulations were again changed and the concession for ex-ration coupon-free wool to knit up for the men and women in the services was withdrawn altogether. It was an anxious moment, but a kind fate intervened. *Punch* office, who had already helped with two generous gifts of wool and a public utility service that stipulated their name should not be divulged, came to the rescue and the Work Party survived. It included in its activities a lively correspondence with College men serving in H.M. Forces, with the dual purpose of discovering their tastes and needs, and of creating a link between the College and her sons abroad, and keeping men informed about each other's activities. A selection of the letters received were passed on to Sweetman, then editor of the *Journal*, for publication, and every man in the Services was sent a copy.

It might be of interest here to note that the workers had no knowledge of the similar efforts undertaken by the Marks Fellowship in the First World War. Like the celebrated Topsy (*Uncle Tom's Cabin*) the War Work Party 'just growed', its activities expanding as the need arose.

In 1940, the College decided to hand over to the Work Party the administration of its Comforts Fund. Books and periodicals had already been distributed on a small scale. This side of the work was now enlarged, and a steadily expanding library service developed. Between November 1942 and November 1943 over six hundred books were sent out.

The Work Party was run on essentially practical lines. There were no surprise parcels. Except for the occasional pair of socks to start a contact with a new correspondent, goods were sent out according to stated needs, and a card index was kept to ensure this. No food parcels could be sent. Stringent rationing at home, due to the submarine menace, forbade this; and in most cases the troops were better off for food than the civilians at home. Original Christmas cards, with a greeting and device suggested by the Work Party, but printed and designed – as a gift to the Comforts Fund – by C. H. Perry, who was an engraver, were sent to each man every year of the war.

The requests received from the men for books and knitted goods – socks were the favourites, with pullovers a good second – were unceasing.

With the help of the Superintendent, Dudley Gill, an arrangement was made with Penguin Books by which the Work Party had a pre-publication choice from their monthly lists; but it was realized this was only a partial solution to the problem (i.e. of obtaining books), for as one Work Party report remarked: 'a clean bound book means much more to the recipient than a paper book, and as far as supplies allow, one is included in every book parcel'. We were helped in this by the Pembridge W.V.S. Depot, who bound books for the Forces. They presented the Work Party with a dozen bound volumes. A special book plate – a gift from Perry's Press – was stuck in every book sent out, to show by whom it had been presented. In the period 1943–4, over five hundred parcels of books and knitted comforts were dispatched, with a personal letter or greeting from the Work Party enclosed in each. In addition a regular flow of personal and individual correspondence in longhand was maintained with all men known to be in the Forces, and a few civilians on war jobs as well. The *Journal* was sent out to all men in the forces by the College. Wrapping materials and postages were heavy items of expenditure, and the cost of the knitting wool rose to between £36 and £40 p.a. By the autumn of 1941 the problem of finance had become acute. In the previous winter College dances, concerts and collections, besides entertainments, etc., undertaken by the Work Party, were the main source of income of the Comforts Fund. In the new circumstances (the blitz on London was at its height) these activities ceased. Thanks however to the generous response of College men to the Old Students' appeal, to donations from friends, and to sundry activities of the ladies of the Work Party, the position

WAR WORK PARTY

by December was much improved, £11 having been handed in to the Bank.

War Work Party Notes. From the Journal. *Trial and Troubles of the Work Party.*

'The Work Party has suffered with the air onslaught and the prolonged hours of blackout. Some members have been evacuated, some had their homes damaged or destroyed. But steps have been taken to meet and overcome the inevitable difficulties, and owing to the ready response and keenness of all members, the work continues and meetings at the College – each month instead of weekly, owing to the changed conditions – are regularly held and well attended. Members of the Work Party evacuated to the country continue their work, posting in their contributions and receiving supplies of wool as before from the Comforts Fund.'

With the introduction of clothes rationing by a system of clothing coupons in 1942 the serious troubles of the Work Party began. The concession of coupon-free wool for knitting up for the services at first allowed, was very soon cancelled by the Board of Trade. The affiliation of the Work Party to the W.V.S. ceased to be of any value. To tide over this crisis, and keep unbroken the continuity of the work, members each gave up some of their personal clothing coupons, and in this way sixty coupons were collected for the immediately necessary purchase of wool. Meanwhile steps were taken by the organizers to seek help elsewhere, which as already related, were successful, and the work continued as before.

Among books given to the Work Party, inevitably, were some that were not likely to prove popular. These were collected, and at intervals, two ladies staggering under the weight of suitcases filled with books, could be seen leaving the College for Foyles bookshop in Charing Cross Road. Foyles, knowing what it was all about, generously paid sixpence a volume. The wealth thus acquired was immediately spent, at Foyles and at the reprint shop across the road, on books more likely to please the prospective recipients. Incidentally the man on the sales counter at Foyles had been a student at the College. But he only remembered it as 'a place where I went to for evening classes', and had obviously never joined in the life of the place.

WAR WORK PARTY

A note in the *Journal* in 1943 relates that 'a lucky swoop on one of Messrs W. H. Smith's bookstalls on the day their monthly quota was put out enabled us to collect forty Penguin and Pelican books on one fortunate day. Worth-while books are becoming increasingly difficult to obtain, but with a mixture of luck and vigilance, strengthened by College support and gifts, somehow the supply has hitherto been maintained'.

Work Party Outing

On May 16th, the Work Party arranged an outing to visit the *Daily Telegraph* Prisoner of War Exhibition at Clarence House. . . . The crowds at the exhibition were considerable, making a detailed and close inspection difficult, but the things that stand out in the memory as a result of what was seen, are the ingenuity of the prisoners, and their courage and indomitable spirit under the intolerably cramped and difficult conditions of their prison life.

Work Party Social and Concert, 1943

'On Friday, August 6th, for the first time since war began, the Maurice Hall was in use by the College, when the Work Party held an afternoon social, and an evening concert for their friends.

'During the afternoon tea – and an excellent tea it was – and 'fun and games' were provided, largely for the purpose of inveigling the unwary into spending money at a 'Bring and Buy' stall. The proceedings were pleasantly enlivened by a selection of light music on the piano played by A. J. Harris and W. H. Barnett.'

The full report of this concert is too long to reproduce here, but it was, in those dark days, a memorable event.

'A gathering reminiscent of a ladies' night in pre-war times attended the concert. Mrs Jopling (Joan Elwes) sang enchantingly a group of English songs, and Captain John de Blois Wack, of the U.S. Army, a professional opera singer persuaded by Mrs Jopling to take part in the programme, sang several solos and joined her later in the programme in a lovely rendering of operatic duets. Mrs Jopling also delighted the audience with a group of Negro spirituals – an altogether entrancing performance. David Cooper, an old favourite at college concerts, played, with perfectly balanced sensitiveness and vigour, a well-chosen and varied selection of classical music, and Lieutenant Genevieve de Lisle of the Canadian Women's Army Corps, a popular radio singer from Quebec, sang charmingly, a group of songs in English and French. A. Harris gave a selection of Strauss waltzes at the piano, and the proceedings terminated with community singing, "God save the King", and, in the good old College tradition, "Auld Lang Syne".'

In 1944 a brief account of Work Party activities appears in the Council's Report.

The autumn number of the *Journal* in the same year describes 'The Summer Party that was held in the common-room that met with considerable success. A garden table, laden with flowers – for members most generously denuded their gardens for the occasion – provided a gay touch of colour and made the room fragrant with summer scents. The flowers were eventually sold and prizes given for the best bunch of roses.

'A sales table provided something in the nature of a scramble, which was a change from the daily shopping queues.

'This function was attended by a number of College folk and their families, including many service members and one returned prisoner of war.'

Some Fragments to illustrate the Variety of Work Party Correspondence and Demands

From Gunner R. L. Green, Field Regt., R.A.

'At the moment I am in Iceland and although it makes a change from England, I find it a very dull country. I have just received the invitation to the Luncheon (Old Students, Christmas) but as you can see it would take a lot of persuading to get the Colonel to give me leave. . . . I should like very much to attend!'

From L/C Tonge, Home Forces, 1942.

'I find myself in a position where a knowledge of the Welsh language would be very useful. Could you tell me if there is a school which runs correspondence courses in this language – or perhaps you have one of your own? . . . Do you have a postal tuition department, and if so, would you be so kind as to send me a brochure?'

WAR WORK PARTY

We did our best to find him a Welsh course through various inquiries. The 'correspondence course' was a good idea, but alas, wishful thinking. Londoners were otherwise occupied during the blitz! But thanks to the generous offer of Mr Evan Jones, of Cardiff University, the matter was informally arranged and he got his 'course in the Welsh language!'

Poems by Crabbe, the works of Bertram Russell, were among book requests sent to the Work Party. On one occasion a client asked for a book on Esperanto! This we were able to supply. A 'log book' and one on Trigonometry were among the less usual requests. These items give a glimpse of the variety of of requests received.

And for the second time, a recipient of a Work Party parcel, writing to acknowledge the contents remarks, 'they were most useful, especially the (two) pullovers (but) I have ten men – that will mean eight more pullovers'.

The following insoluble conundrum – was it a 'leg pull'? – also reached the Work Party. 'I had a letter from a student which I have mislaid. He signs himself "Bill Hart". but that was not his proper name. I forget that. Apparently he mixed my name with that of somebody else, as he says I was in Switzerland with him in 1938 – I have never been to Switzerland. Could you get in touch with him and inform him?'

The letter was published in the *Journal*, the only possible way to deliver its message.

XX

THE PLAYING FIELD DURING THE WAR

THE reports concerning the Playing Field are scattered through the pages of the wartime numbers of the *Journal*. They have here been gathered together to give a reasonably clear, comprehensive picture of the Playing Field's affairs during the war years.

1939 '... activities on the ground have been curtailed as the Pavilion has been taken over by the Harrow U.D.C. as a rescue and demolition centre.... Fortunately the officer in charge of the centre, Mr Rosier, has done all in his power to make the relations between A.R.P. workers and College members friendly and cordial, and the College has done all in its power to reciprocate this. Tansley (Football Club) had experienced difficulty in arranging matches; there were no league games, but "football matches on the ground between A.R.P. teams and the College team have been frequent, with varying results ... the A.R.P. team have the use of one football pitch. Two concerts have been held in the Pavilion and further social entertainments are planned.'

George Bankes, the vigorous chairman of the Playing Field Committee, came to the Pavilion and harangued the Rescue and Demolition Squad in occupation on 'the College'. The *Journal* thus reports the incident: 'An interesting address on The Working Men's College given by George Bankes on

February 17th was well received by members of the Rescue and Demolition Squad at Edgware.'

Another valuable contact was made by G. Bankes on March 17th, when he spoke, again at the Playing Field, to the Demolition Squad at Edgware on 'Law – the Right of Public Meetings, etc.'

A little later, unlinked with any previous comment, with sudden irresponsible gaiety, the *Journal* produces this:

'*Full Marks* to the student who wrote to the A.R.P. section, "I regret I am unable to attend tonight as I have my class at The Working Men's College."'

Report on Tansley Football Club, from the Journal, *January 1940*

'At the outbreak of hostilities the College Playing Field and Pavilion were taken over by the Harrow A.R.P. Services, and it appeared likely that College football would have to be suspended for the time being.

'However, George Bankes put in some valuable work on behalf of the Club, and it was finally arranged that Tansley should have the use of one football pitch each week. The Nemean League Competition had already been suspended, and it was decided by the Tansley Committee to continue activities by arranging friendly games for two elevens each week.'

Report on the Playing Field, 1940

'During the summer months the Playing Field was used by the three College Clubs. The Bowls Club in particular had a successful season and the number of men using the Green was very encouraging. The Club owes a great deal to E. McShee and the other officials of the Club for the trouble they took. It was particularly pleasant to see members of the Rescue and Demolition Squads taking part in some of the matches on the Green.'

One gathers from the accounts in the *Journal* that the Tennis Club also was surviving, in spite of the difficulties, and 'had a satisfactory season. During several week-ends there was a good attendance of members, but the plans for transforming two grass courts into hard courts, for which funds had been raised, had to be abandoned for the period of the war, and the money returned to the donors.'

THE PLAYING FIELD DURING THE WAR

Report on the Cricket Club

In announcing their match arrangements for the 1940 season the *Journal* remarks: 'it is hoped that tea will be available in the Pavilion, thanks to the co-operation of the A.R.P. squads. . . . Changing accommodation will be available in the Pavilion, but members and visitors will need to be careful not to disturb the equipment of the A.R.P. or this privilege will be withdrawn.' Two friendly games were arranged each week. 'The use of the pitches on the Playing Field being considerably restricted, the opportunity has been taken to give the ground a rest, which it sorely needs after ten years' continuous use. The drains across the football pitches are being relaid and extended – as a result it is hoped that the ground will be drier during the rainy seasons than it has been hitherto.'

There was a Garden Party at the Playing Field in 1940 that was run in conjunction with the Harrow Rescue and Demolition Squad, who occupied the Pavilion.

In contrast to the 1939 Garden Party, the event was marred by rain. There were, as might have been expected, fewer entries than usual for the major events, though the local police entered a team for the tug-of-war. In the veterans' race, the *Journal* relates: 'George Bankes ran extremely well, and would surely have gained a place had he removed his hat and mackintosh before running!' The music for the afternoon was provided by the College Musical Society.

It was the last Garden Party for the duration of the war.

General Position

The general situation of the Playing Field at the end of hostilities is summed up in this note:

'The Playing Field has benefitted substantially both from the generosity and the wise economies of George Bankes (who died suddenly in 1944 in the changing-rooms of the Playing Field, at the age of 42). His name will be remembered in honour and affection by the generation of College men who knew him as a teacher, an enthusiastic member of the football and cricket teams and, in the best sense, a common-room man. It was in the main thanks to his care and forethought that the end of the war found the Playing Field with a balance of about £500 available to replace equipment lost and destroyed in the war years.'

THE PLAYING FIELD DURING THE WAR

Position of the Playing Field, 1944

'War conditions of course have restricted activity, but successful efforts have been made to maintain the Tennis and Bowls Clubs, though the membership is sadly reduced. The cricket club has arranged half-day matches on Sunday afternoons. But even cricket had its hazards. Dudley Gill recalls a cricket match in 1944 when he and the rest of the team went flat on their faces while a "flying bomb" passed overhead, to explode a short distance farther on. The game continued.'

The Results of being 'Taken Over' by Civil Defence

'The College has agreed with Middlesex County Council on the proper amount to be paid by them in compensation for the damage to College property in the pavilion.'

XXI

DUDLEY GILL TAKES A LOOK AT THE COLLEGE

~~~~~~~~~~~~~~~~~~~~~~~~~~~~~~

DUDLEY GILL came first to the College in 1923 as a teacher of Physical Geography.... He undertook with success the big task of rearranging and relabelling the valuable geological collection in the Lionel Jacob Museum. From 1933 to 1936 he taught mathematics and in 1936–7 was College tutor in what was then known as Section A; in 1938–9 he taught Latin. He succeeded C. Chapman as Superintendent in 1942.

'In 1942 I took up my appointment as what was then called Superintendent of Working Men's College, and with my wife and family moved into the flat in the new wing. We arrived during a lull in the blitz, but things soon began to warm up.

'One night, when a bomb fell all too close to the College, destroying the row of small shops and cottages that stood opposite, the Maurice Hall assumed again the grim role assigned to it at the beginning of the air attack on London, and became a mortuary; this time combining with that office the no less grim but more satisfying work of a First Aid Post. Little do those who see the hall now, gaily decorated for dances, resplendent in white cloths and gleaming cutlery for the annual Old Students' Supper, or more soberly celebrating such occasions as Founders' Night, realize what scenes it could evoke.

'It was after this catastrophe that Pont, the caretaker, was on the roof, struggling single-handed to cover gaping skylights with tarpaulin, when he heard the telephone bell ring. Swift descent was impossible, but a voice floated up to him from below demanding to know why he was so slow in answering the call. Pont's reply is unprintable!

'The Studies Committee had been dissolved at the beginning of the war, classes were few and teachers, through the circumstances of their war duties, liable to be erratic in their attendance. Thus it would fall to the Superintendent to play many parts and give instruction, as best he might, in a variety of subjects. Apart from these efforts the duties of the Superintendent in war time could be summed up as anything that needed to be done. I have taken my turn with Pont in scrubbing passages and stoking boilers, and was called upon by the Executive to convey to a particularly obnoxious character who had been haunting the wartime common-room, that he would no longer be admitted to the College. As he was an extremely large aggressive man, weighing about fifteen stone, I felt somewhat nervous – unnecessarily as it turned out. He shouted, 'Whose nominee are you?' but left without causing any further trouble.

'Throughout the blitz bombs continued to fall unpleasantly near Crowndale Road. On one occasion, returning with my family from a week-end break in the country, I found that the blast from a near miss had torn off a number of doors and windows in the College.

'I inaugurated first-aid repairs – and was only rescued from a large fine or imprisonment by Ellis Franklin. It seems that one may not take such steps in wartime without first filling up the appropriate forms!'

D. M. C. GILL.

Dudley's recollections would be incomplete without mention of his wife Clare, who did so much to assist the smooth running of the domestic side of the College, and laboured unceasingly on behalf of the Work Party.

The Ponts could be prickly if tactlessly handled, but Clare's diplomacy and friendliness ensured happy relations all round.

Chairs would be carried up to the flat, or moved around the common-rooms for fund-raising functions, or refreshments organized in the College; the ladies of the Work Party were given the freedom of the serving-room and a corner of their own to store provisions for the teas at their afternoon meetings, not only without protest, but willingly as though it were a pleasure.

Clare kept herself in the background, but she was, in her quiet way, of inestimable help, and made many friends in the College.

MAJOR GENERAL SIR F. B. MAURICE, K.C.M.G., C.B.,
D.LITT., LL.D.
Principal 1922–33

THE RIGHT HON. LORD GREENE
Principal 1936–44

XXII

COLLEGE PERSONALITIES

Some Important People, 1939–45
SIR FREDERICK MAURICE, great grandson of the Founder, became Principal of the College between the two Great Wars. He had charm, wisdom and humanity, was approachable and kindly, with wide understanding. He will go down to history as one of the great principals of the College. After he had retired from the principalship he became Chairman of the Corporation, and continued to serve on the Council till failing health and old age compelled him to give up.

He was succeeded as Principal in 1933 by Sir Arnold Wilson, tall, dark, soldierly; sincere, conscientious and serious in his approach to his duties in the College, he remained somehow in many ways always a stranger there. He was of those who had believed a *rapprochement* with Germany possible, and had felt a certain sympathy with the vigorous Nazi patriotism. It was characteristic that when war broke out, with its terrible exposure of Nazi bad faith and savagery, he recognized his error, and immediately, in a gesture of penitence, at the age of 55, joined the R.A.F. and flew as an air gunner in a heavy bomber. He was killed in May 1940 when the machine in which he was flying was shot down behind the German lines.

His successor as Principal, Sir Wilfrid Greene, a distinguished barrister, later to be appointed Master of the Rolls, was a brilliant, cultured, intellectual, but very human personality. Like Sir Frederick Maurice, he made it his business to become a

SOME IMPORTANT PEOPLE

familiar figure in the common-room as well as at the Council table. It was regretted on all sides when pressure of work, after his appointment as Master of the Rolls, compelled him to retire from the College.

Sir Wilfrid Eady, who succeeded him in 1942, was a civil servant with an exceptionally high reputation. A scholarly man, regarded in his own sphere as expert in handling difficult human

SIR WILFRID EADY K.C.M.G., K.C.B., K.B.E.
Principal 1944-1955

SOME IMPORTANT PEOPLE

situations and problems, he seemed an especially fortunate choice. He worked with great devotion for the college for a number of years, his tenure of office embracing the centenary celebrations, when Her Majesty the Queen and Prince Philip honoured it with a visit.

The Vice-Principal throughout the years of the Second World War was Frank Gahan, a Canadian barrister who had been called to the English bar. Sincere, hardworking, wise, with the welfare of the College very near to his heart, calm and thoughtful, he was the ideal Vice-Principal for those troubled times. He was loyally supported in his work for the College by his wife.

The Bursar was Ellis Franklin. It is not fitting that I, his wife, should attempt to evaluate his service to the College. But I can say that I know how largely it loomed in his thought, and how deep was his concern not only to do all that was possible in the present, but to prepare wisely for the post-war future of the College. And I know the large amount of time that he gave to it out of a life complicated by his war work as a part-time civil servant, and the added complexities of his professional duties in the city, with two partners in the army, and one enfeebled and semi-retired at the age of 80. I know of his great love for the place, of the many friends he had made there, and of his pleasure in the life of the common-room.

George Bankes, in the best sense a common-room man, was on the executive and the Council of the College, wartime chairman of the Old Students' Club, and the energetic Chairman of the Playing Field Committee. As these pages show, the Playing Field, founded by the enterprise of Ellis Franklin, owes much to the care, generosity and foresight of George Bankes during the war years.

1941 saw the death of Charles Wright, student, teacher, benefactor, and for over fifty years a member of the College. His generous gifts to the Endowment Fund and Playing Field Appeals, launched by Ellis Franklin, not only justified the latter's faith in attaining their targets, but ensured the success of appeals that were sent out in the face of many dismal prophecies of failure. Charles Wright's life was a success story – the poor boy, one of a family of eight children, starting out to work at the age of thirteen in a warehouse, earning 5s. 9d. a week, who gained his education at the College. When through

SOME IMPORTANT PEOPLE

dogged hard work, wealth and an assured position were his – he became a respected member of Lloyd's Shipping Insurance – he repaid with affection, service, and gifts from his fortune, the debt that he felt that he owed to the College.

Another old student who owed his successful progress to the College was Herbert Heather, a director of Bradbury Agnew, printer, and publisher of *Punch*. Unspoilt by success, he maintained the connection with the College throughout his life, and always held for it 'a warm spot in his heart'. He died in 1943.

War work and business commitments, closely interwoven, kept G. F. A. Burgess away from the College over most of the war years. Teacher, Vice-Principal for four years between the wars, and Chairman of the Corporation in succession to Maurice; Chairman of the Old Students' Club after the Second World War, and always a familiar figure in the common-room, it is right that he should be remembered here.

There is an account in the *Journal* of a Student Teachers' Meeting at which he was the speaker. The substance of his remarks is typical of the man. He spoke on what he called 'the Five Traditions of the College, namely, the traditions of Service, of Liberal Education, of Fellowship, of Freedom of Thought, and Voluntary Service'. On service he observed 'the extraordinary thing is that people always turned up, and they have been turning up since 1854. . . . Ellis Franklin used to watch the appointments in the Civil Service, who got new jobs in the Government Departments. He got on to X and the telephone conversation was "I have spoken to him already and of course he is coming to the college . . ." The great advantage of the voluntary system is that teachers not only want to educate students, but want to educate themselves. I tried to teach economics here, and I learned more about economics in trying to teach, than I did at Cambridge – I got to know more about life.'

His professional work increasingly took Burgess for long periods abroad. But whenever his work allowed, he returned to the service of the College. His last task was to pilot harmoniously through the Council, the intricacies of the new Constitution of the College in 1963. He died in the summer of that year at the early age of 60.

XXIII

'NO MEMORIAL...'

'No Memorial...'

To attempt to give a comprehensive account of the dominant personalities in the College between 1939 and 1945 – apart from those holding high office, who figure on another page – would be a hopeless task, for there were many. Some names are legendary and will live in men's memories as long as the College survives. It is, one feels, the lesser luminaries who should be remembered here.

One thinks of Ted Gann, limping and genial, a cobbler by trade – his infirmity making service in the Forces out of the question – who undertook all boot repairs without charge, for the refugees thronging the W.V.S. Depot in the basement of the College. Sweetman, the editor of the *Journal*, gentle, unassuming, always helpful. A busy man with a heart infirmity so pronounced he could never go to bed, but must spend his nights sitting up in a chair. He lived to pass the strong man's span of 'three score years and ten' and died an octogenarian, after the war.

Dimes, already by 1919 the College librarian – a small rock-like individual who continued, seemingly unchanged, through the uneasy years between the wars, and survived the Second World War, a splendid anachronism in the modern world.

Of him a student wrote: 'H. B. Dimes comes in about 6 p.m. The library opens, and he shuts himself away in the library where he has worked for twenty-five years; he has Friday off.'

'NO MEMORIAL...'

Dimes – that little, round shouldered, mildly pugnacious yet endearing figure, so familiar in the college for so many years – was an institution. An out-and-out traditionalist, he lived for the College in general, and the library in particular.

I well remember my husband when he first became Vice-Principal, knowing how anxious I was to help if it were possible, coming home happily one day with the news he had found a job at the College for me – the books in the library wanted hoovering. Delightedly we went up one evening together and he installed me in the library, busy with Hoover and books. In comes H. B. Dimes, polite, but implacable, 'Sorry, no ladies are allowed in the library.' Exit Mrs Franklin, ignominiously, to wait for her husband on the old wooden bench in the hall!

The College has moved a little since – Dimes would be horrified to see once every week, two volunteers from the Ladies' Association helping to check the books in his library!

The caretakers, Mr and Mrs Pont, grappled with everything, from bombs to the innumerable demands of Civil Defence workers of both sexes; and last, but not least, the Old Students' Club luncheons, with no one to assist their labours but well intentioned amateurs, a couple of cleaners, and the redoubtable 'Ernie', the serving-room boy; at once the benevolent spirit and the terror of his domain – ready to render any service if handled the right way, but with a devastating cockney riposte if ruffled.

Neither C. H. Perry, nor E. McShee, who taught shorthand, would thank one for praise among the 'lesser luminaries' of the College, but in their different ways each gave it loyal service, and were of inestimable help to the Work Party.

Before, between and after the two great wars, C. H. Perry was a notable figure in the College. An eccentric, with a rough tongue when he was angered, and a long memory for an insult, imagined or real, he had strong prejudices; but to those persons or causes that found favour in his sight, he was unfailingly generous and kind. A typical Perry story is of his bringing to the College two bags of apples from his garden. One he gave to Mrs Gill for whom he had a considerable respect, 'They are good,' he said, 'that,' indicating the second bag, 'is for Mr X ... they're *all bad!*' He was an engraver and made many gifts of his work

'NO MEMORIAL . . .'

for College purposes. The picture of the College that used to adorn the cover of the *Journal* was designed and presented by C. H. Perry. The brother-in-law of Alice Perry, once a soubrette of the D'Oyly Carte Opera Company, his rendering of the Policeman's Song from the 'Pirates of Penzance' and other base solos from the Savoy Operas, were indispensable items at College concerts and sing-songs. He was a pillar of the Musical Society, and for some years secretary of the Old Students' Club.

Two friends of the College, whose sons – both students – were in the forces, deserve recalling here. Throughout the war, Mr and Mrs Badger, who owned a small newspaper shop in Crowndale Road, kept open house for College men. Their shop was bombed, one of their sons, Ron, was killed in a flying accident in the R.A.F. while teaching men to fly – their spirit remained unbroken. Any service they could render the College was eagerly undertaken, and the welcome in the little room behind the shop, for all connected with the College, continued warm and cheerful.

These are but a few of the many who could claim they deserve to be remembered. Prominent in their day, most of them unknown to succeeding generations, they exemplify the spirit of all those who were active in the College at that time. In remembering these, one pays tribute to so many more.

Two Eccentrics

The College had its share of eccentrics.

Barnett Freedman was introduced by Sir William Rothenstein. Physically small, with rounded shoulders and a powerful head and strong features, in character dynamic and full of enthusiasm, he was a popular and successful teacher of the art classes.

He became one of the 'war artists' recruited by the Government, and was in France when the evacuation was ordered at Dunkirk. The *Evening Standard* of July 3rd, 1940, relates how 'one of the paintings on view at the exhibition by war artists . . . at the National Gallery had been saved from Boulogne under heavy machine-gun fire and bombing attacks.'

'Barnett Freedman was given orders to embark during the embarkation from Boulogne. His kit, containing eight works, was placed in a ship. . . . But Mr Freedman determined to

'NO MEMORIAL...'

rescue his last picture 'Aircraft-Run in Construction at Arras', which was in his hotel.

'Disobeying orders, he dashed down the gangway and rushed through the streets, which were filled with refugees. Airplanes were machine-gunning and bombing the whole time. When he reached his hotel, Mr Freedman found that everyone had been evacuated – 'but I got my picture!'

'He ran back to the harbour. His ship had left with his kit aboard. While waiting for another vessel he helped to unload an ammunition ship.'

Though it took the War Office a month to trace the eight paintings that had sailed without the artist, eventually they were found, and with the rescued picture, they now hang in the National Gallery.

Freedman found the atmosphere of the war immensely stimulating. 'I want,' he said, 'to express (on canvas) what is a unique period in English history . . . the rush to build fortifications . . . the atmosphere of the whole race getting ready to repel the invader.'

'The French,' he told a newspaper reporter when discussing the Boulogne episode, 'were amazed to see on the battlefield an English officer walking about doing paintings. They were impressed.'

Freedman's work has left its impact. His character was vigorous, his health frail. He died while still comparatively young a few years after the end of the war.

In a very different category was Eric Cooke, enthusiastic member of the Furnival Cycling Club. He spent much of the war years on two wheels, and through the Work Party kept well in touch with the College, even calling there occasionally, as it were, between rides. He kept the Furnival Cycling Club alive, organizing rides, regardless of all obstacles, with the few elderly enthusiasts still available.

The end of the war saw him, loaded rather like the White Knight, astride his (two wheeled) steed, setting out to cycle to New Zealand, where he was proposing to make his home.

A strange arrival for an immigrant – on a bicycle!

XIV

MORE NOTES FROM THE JOURNAL

The Classes in Wartime
'COLLEGE classes in wartime may be few in number and small in size, but the pleasure they give to students and teachers is considerable. This is undoubtedly so in the two classes which differ from the others in being more speculative and more discursive. These are the classes in Citizenship and English Literature, which are held in the Bernard Pitt Room (No. 10) on Wednesday evenings at 6.30 and 7.45.

'... In both classes the students have quite as much to say as the teachers, and every encouragement is given to an exchange of views on matters in which tastes and opinions differ. Each evening's work, while it is related to what has been previously studied, can be enjoyed in itself. A warm welcome is therefore extended to all College men who are interested, even if they are unable to attend regularly, to visit one or both classes on any Wednesday and join in the lively discussion.'

Shorthand and Russian Classes
'Good work done by McShee with his shorthand class during the raid period 1940–41 was an inspiration to those able to attend the class. Russian and English classes were started in October to meet the demands of College men. ... The Russian class began with a handful of students ... it increased in numbers. ... Not a minute was wasted in the class. ... The progress made has surprised the teacher ... who says he has

concentrated a year's lessons into the few months the class has been in existence. . . . A pupil when asked what method was used replied: 'We call it Russian without tears. We are driven so hard we haven't time to cry."'

In 1940 the *Journal* printed 'An Open Letter to Any New Student' which is as applicable today as when it was written. 'To be a true college man,' the writer declares, 'you must be a student. If you don't want to study, the College does not want you. . . . You *must* use the common- and coffee-rooms and drift into the Social and Club life. . . .' It is a long letter written by a College man, but those two sentences are the heart of it. With the modern tendency to casualness and a too ready acceptance of easier standards, it is not inappropriate to recall what the College has meant to successive generations of students and teachers alike.

In a lighter vein, but still with a significance of what the College stands for in the minds and sentiments of its members, is this version of the legend of 'The Old School Tie'. A student on holiday writes: 'Do you know a chap named Barry? I met him while on holiday. He looked at my tie, I looked at his. He grabbed me by the hand . . .'

In 1941 the *Journal* gives the information that the College now is H.Q. of G. and N. zone of the Home Guard. Captain the hon. E. Eliot* and Charles Hambourg are on the staff . . .'

Friday Evenings at the College

On Friday evenings during the war students were invited to gather round the fire in the Superintendent's room. Everyone who came on that evening signed a book, and left messages for those whom they wished to meet. A College man describes one of these evenings: 'Woodruffe and Ginever engaged in chess . . . the Editor (of the *Journal*) making notes. . . . Charles Hambourg, not waving a conductor's baton as I had always previously seen him, but beaming over a succulent dish Pont had just placed before him; and not displaying his braces as when rehearsing the orchestra, but looking very large and fine in his Home Guard uniform.' The writer then names numerous other College men encountered that evening and continues: 'In the office I saw Dimes (Librarian) bent over what I assumed to be

---

* Member of the College orchestra.

College accounts, and at that moment a stalwart figure walked – no, not walked, strode in, and without any preamble picked up a sheet of figures he seemed to comprehend at a glance. . . . Truly the Bursar looked as fit as ever, despite his having to keep one foot in the city and the other in Westminster, for it is rumoured that after leaving the Bank at midday he spends the afternoon at Westminster on matters of Civil Defence.

'Eyes brightened all round when Bankes came in – he is another man who is doing all he can to keep the College life going in these difficult times. Well, instead of finding the College moribund, I found it full of life . . .'

Some small items of personal news find their place among the jottings in the *Journal*. A note congratulates A. Smith (a member of the College orchestra) on the promotion of his son Cyril, who is serving in the R.A.F., to the rank of Squadron Leader. 'Cyril Smith has flown on sixty operational flights, is in the Pathfinder Force, and has been awarded the D.S.O.'

'David Franklin, eldest son of our Bursar, having volunteered to join Airborne Forces, is now (1943) back from North Africa, undergoing the necessary training. He finds jumping from aeroplanes a most pleasing and exhilarating experience. He was temporarily in the same company (R.A.S.C.) as R. H. Jerrold, College student and son of an old student.'

'The Bursar's second son, Colin, is in South Africa. After four months as a rating in a destroyer he is now (1942) a naval cadet, training at the naval depot H.M.S. *Good Hope* at Port Elizabeth, where another college man serving in the Royal Navy, J. A. Clements, also underwent an officers training course.'

In his first 'ship', H.M.S. *Collingwood*,* a naval camp in Hampshire, Colin had met a College student, L/S/B/A Harris, who was serving in the same ship.

Bun Pence Appeal

F. Jennings has achieved the remarkable feat of collecting thirty-two shillings in 'bun pence' for the Ladies War Work Party funds. The bun pence idea, originally advanced by C. H. Perry, has met outstanding success and brought many pounds to the Work Party. The record for one year was £20.

* All naval training camps are known as 'ships'.

MORE NOTES FROM THE JOURNAL

News Item from a Report of the Council Meeting, 24th June, 1942
'The railings in front of the College had originally been scheduled as unnecessary by the local authorities. They were designed by the late W. D. Caroe, who devoted his fees for the College extension, to providing them as his gift to the College. When the circumstances were explained, the local authorities willingly removed them from the schedule.'

More Personal News from the Journal
'Congratulations to our Bursar, Ellis A. Franklin, on having conferred on him the honour O.B.E. (for his war work at the Home Office).'

'College listeners no doubt recognized the voice of James Laver, recently broadcasting on the subject of "War Savings". A civil servant at the Victoria and Albert Museum, Laver was doomed, as his war job, to go up and down the country propaganding for war savings on behalf of the Government. He first came to the College in response to the letter the Vice-Principal (then Ellis Franklin) sent to all new-comers to the Civil Service. . . . He became a highly successful and individual director of the College art classes, and an ever welcome guest and witty speaker at College functions.'

A note from the Work Party relates that: 'In the last few weeks letters have come from two College men who have been stationed in Colombo, Ceylon. It has also been discovered that two men who are prisoners of war have been placed in the same camp. In each of these cases steps were taken immediately by the Work Party, writing by air mail to each individual to inform him of the other's proximity. It is hoped by this means the men may be able to meet.'

Old Students' Club

The old Students' Club meetings during the war were held on Saturday afternoons. Ladies were invited. In 1942 the series included talks by the Bursar, Ellis Franklin on 'Finance', and by 'Sir Frederick Maurice, K.C.M.G. [subject not stated] who will unveil a portrait of Sir Arnold Wilson, presented by the artist S. T. C. Weeks.'

The Bursar called his talk 'Economic Hopes and Fears'. Among the hopes he included 'full employment, with good housing, bearing in mind that the war is not being fought to build a better Britain, but is one for survival. . . . In all our plans priority should be given to those who fought this war, and this includes the citizens of London'. Planned production was another necessity . . . another hope was for improved education. . . . The Bursar also explored the question of how the Government was able to finance the war – always a mystery to laymen. He gave a most lucid explanation of just how it works . . . the discussion that followed was full and varied.

A brief summary of the views expressed in his talk is given here because they are so characteristic; his common-sense realistic approach, combined with practical sympathy and insight.

College Horticultural Show

As one of their fund raising and social functions, the Work Party in 1943 had planned a horticultural show, of flowers and produce from their own and College members' gardens. It was a new and promising idea . . . *but* . . . planning in time of war has many hazards. . . .

Note from the Journal *in the Late Summer of 1943*

'As we go to Press a blast has again severely damaged College doors, windows, ceilings, etc., and it is not certain that repairs can be made in time for the Horticultural Show and the Art Class Exhibition, which were postponed till September.'

College Notes

'Corpl. A. Hitchen, of the R.A.F., just back from the Middle East, visited the College a little while ago. He had a warm welcome on his first night home – two "buzz-bombs" landed near his house, and so he was soon numbered among the many of us who have had to sweep up glass and pick out pieces of it from the furniture. And he had been having such a peaceful time in Cairo! Whilst there he had had to climb up and down one of the Pyramids as part of his work! (He helped set up and operate a radio-location unit on the Pyramid during the big Conference at Cairo.)'

'Sub-Lieut. "Dick" White is in charge of a tug, and engaged on mine-laying. Being completely in charge of his outfit, and with a motley crew, he is thoroughly enjoying the life. He visited the College during a spell of leave in May.'

Another 'note' gives the information that 'Sub-Lieut. Dick (goalkeeper) White, R.N., was sent over to Normandy on a special job. On the night of his arrival there the Army was forced to give ground and Dick had an uncomfortable time for a few hours. Some time later he was ordered to go on to Caen, which he was told had been taken by the Canadians. He was given a staff car and was soon *en route*. When he arrived at a damaged bridge just before the town, he got out, had a look round and decided to retrace his steps. Whilst inquiring the position of a soldier, a number of mortar shells came over and blew off the roof of his car – the Germans had not seen Dick's orders and unsportingly still held half of the town. He discovered the damaged bridge was the middle of the battle area and wisely decided to return to base. By this time mortar shells were plentiful and a Canadian soldier was wounded by one. Dick took him to a dressing station (and subsequently visited him in hospital in England, where he's making a good recovery). However, this is not quite the end of Dick's story, because on his first night back in London, a flying-bomb came down near his house. It threw his bed about, blew the windows and window-frames in and the ceiling down on him. Apart from a few cuts Dick was not badly hurt. Still, he took a very poor view of the war when a few nights later another flying-bomb fell within a few yards of the first. Dick is now undecided whether to stay in London or go back to France.'

Extract from a News Item Published in the Public Press: 'Penniless' Army Freed a City, 1944

'A "penniless" British Army liberated Brussels.

'Its advance was so swift that Pay Corps field cashiers with the advanced forces had received no Belgian currency.

'So Captain S. G. Hale,* attached as cashier to a Guards armoured division, called at headquarters of the Banque Nationale de Belgique and explained the position.

'Directors were summoned, champagne and cigars were produced, then, refusing all security, the directors unlocked their

---

* Captain Hale is a College member. In civilian life he works at a merchant bank in the city of London.

vaults and handed over 3,500,000 francs (about £20,000) and told Captain Hale that he could come back for more if it was wanted.'

By Christmas time 1944, a jubilant note of optimism and looking forward to happier times, well illustrated by the paragraph quoted below, has crept into the *Journal*.

1944. '"As it was in days of yore . . ." During evenings, Saturday afternoons, Sunday mornings, and on occasional free days, the coffee room, serving-room and Superintendent's Office are being redecorated by a band of volunteer workers, among whom we see the Superintendent, Cooke, Taylor and Son, (F. M.) Barry, Ramage, Lewin and Swann. In doing a good job they are earning our warmest thanks, and are preparing (not prematurely, we hope), for the return of the men from the Forces.'

In the autumn of 1944 the Art Class held an exhibition at Foyles Galleries. It was well attended.

A *Journal* note in 1945 states: 'It is learned that Monsieur Tissier [French Teacher at The Working Men's College] who was caught in Vichy France is once more back in England, and has visited the College. We extend to him a cordial welcome home.'

XXV

COLLEGE COUNCIL AND EMERGENCY COMMITTEE REPORTS

AT the Council Meeting in June 1939, 'Sir Frederick Maurice moved that the name of W. D. Caroe* be inserted in the Benefactor's Panel of the Honours Boards. The Bursar seconded the motion, and both referred to the long years of service Caroe had given to the College, and his generosity in planning the present building' (for which he had accepted no fee).

'The Bursar then presented the accounts for the year 1938-9.' The point of interest in these being that 'the income from fees was less than in the previous years, due to the unsettled conditions prevailing at the beginning of the session.

A nice understatement referring to the year of Munich!

Council Meeting, November 1939

Emergency Measures.

The most important result of the Council Meeting of November 29th, 1939, was the appointment of an emergency committee to control College affairs generally. This committee, which consists of the ex-officio members of the Executive Committee and eight members of Council, was appointed 'to hold office until the meeting of Council in November 1940, *or* until the meeting of the Council next after the College is able to resume

---

* W. D. Caroe was the architect of the present building and his son, A. Caroe, continues to advise the College in that capacity.

its normal work, whichever shall happen first.... The committee has power to co-opt. By this means the College is assured of a working committee consisting of members who are able regularly to attend meetings to control the affairs of the College during the present emergency. The following are the elected members: G. Bankes, S. Burge, R. Chaynes, H. Dimes, J. Hughes, R. Morrison, C. H. Perry, J. Shiker.

'*Officers*. The present officers, i.e. F. Gahan (Vice-Principal), Ellis Franklin (Bursar), H. Dimes (Librarian), and the Auditors were reappointed for the year 1940.

'There being no longer, during the period of the emergency, a Studies Committee, no chairman of that committee was appointed.

'H. Feingold, in a motion of which due notice had been given, urged a plea for the admission of contributions on controversial matters which he suggested would increase interest in the *Journal*. W. C. Woodruffe seconded the motion, saying that he felt that the *Journal* lacked that interest which a spirit of healthy controversy would, in his opinion, give it. The expression healthy controversy was accepted by Council who was anxious, to judge by the comments made on both sides, that the *Journal* should not become an instrument of political controversy or of petty bickering between correspondents, and in this spirit the motion was carried by a majority vote.'

Council Meeting, March 1940

The Council Meeting of March 1940, presided over by Sir Wilfred Greene, began by expressing its appreciation of the work of A. J. W. Walker, B.Sc., College Fellow, for six years assistant superintendent of the College. This office ceased on February 29th, 1940.

The urgency to prepare a programme of classes for the next session is stressed, and the anxiety of the Council that the College should be as active as possible in present circumstances. ...

'During the war the policy has been to start a class whenever students are available. There are now nineteen classes which will be continued until the beginning of July. Unfortunately present conditions make for irregularity in attendance.

'The College is giving valuable and much-appreciated help to the Service of Youth Movement. Accommodation in the

College has been placed at the disposal of the Samuel Lithgow Social Centre, and each week about twenty boys, under proper supervision, use for physical training and games, the gymnasium and the Maurice Hall. Your committee hope that many of the boys from the Centre will later become College students. . . .

'Professor Chorley and J. Currie have been added to the Emergency Committee that will review the whole educational position and consider what improvements on past work can be made . . . the question of possible courses of study systematically planned to cover three or four years was raised in these deliberations. The Committee was assured it was not proposed entirely to change the system of enrolment for individual classes.

'The College is endeavouring to keep in close touch with all those members who are serving in the Forces. Their efforts are assisted by the W.M.C. Ladies' War Work Party.'

Standstill. Newspaper headings stating 'Evening Education at a Standstill' did not apply to the College whose classes reopened as soon as the ban on holding evening classes was lifted.

'There were many difficulties – such as providing adequate safety during air raids. Our air-raid shelter in the basement has, fortunately, not had to be used. We express appreciation for the assistance given in the work to provide protection. The Bursar, Ellis Franklin, and his family, as well as members of the Executive, came down to fill sandbags, and among others F. Stubbs and J. Shiker gave much assistance during week-ends.'

Sympathy is expressed by the *Journal* reporter 'with the renters whose lockers in the basement have been demolished to provide room for air-raid shelter'. It was noted that a gift of 100 books for the library had been received from N. Hardy, a former teacher.

Council Meeting, June 1940

The policy of starting a class whenever a sufficient number of students could be found for it, and of continuing as long as the students were prepared to attend, was given fresh emphasis. Members of Council and old students were also urged to 'make a point of spending an evening in the common-room as often as they could, for the common-room is an essential part of the education that the College offers. . . .' Among the detailed plans for the next Session were special short courses in mathematics. Tribute was paid to Charles Wright, old student, College Fellow and benefactor of the College, and to W. D'A. Stenning, teacher and student, whose deaths were reported. The Council recorded its profound sense of loss.

At this time of intense night bombing and erratic duty hours for many individuals, some of the College classes were held in the afternoon and even on Saturdays.

Emergency Committee, 1941

There is no report in the *Journal* of any Council Meeting in 1941, but a full account by the Emergency Committee of the state of the College in the early phases of the war is given.

'During the session 1939–40,' the report informs its readers, 'eighteen classes were run and the number of class entries was 286; the number of students joining the College was 461 including 204 Old Students; a number of students permitted to take out Old Students' tickets were unable to do so because wartime duties prevented them from regular class attendance.'

Reference is made in this account to the Ladies Work Party and to the Old Students' Luncheon on 28th December, 1940.

Since September 1940, the report points out, 'the intensive night bombing of London has reduced College activities to the smallest proportion . . . the decision to reduce the age limit of admitting students from 17 to 16 years did not meet with the anticipated success. . . .' The Old Students' Club is urged to be more active and hold as many meetings as possible – only one meeting was held in the Session under review.*

'It is impossible,' the report concludes, 'to make any prophecy as to future developments, but it is clear that the survival of the College will depend on the answer to the question how much each individual member is prepared to do for it. . . .'

Council Meeting, June 1942

At this meeting C. H. Perry was congratulated by the Council 'on the completion of fifty years membership of the College . . .' The report of the Executive 'deeply concerned with the

---

* This was remedied in the following session when eight meetings were held.

problems of the future' was read and earnestly discussed. ...
'The Executive Committee has considered and is still considering steps to be taken before the end of the war to ensure that when peace comes, the College can resume its full activities in circumstances that will again enable it to take its place in the forefront of adult education. . . . The Council also expressed appreciation and gratitude to the staff for the willingness and success with which they have undertaken responsibilities which would not normally fall to them.' Feingold moved a series of resolutions to affect changes in the constitution of the council that were referred to the Executive Committee for consideration and report.

Council Meeting, July 1943

Session, 1943-4.

This commenced on September 20th, with an announcement of a total of thirteen classes. The subjects chosen included Arithmetic, Mathematics, Geography, Art, French, German, English, Russian and Citizenship. 'It is hoped that as many as possible will avail themselves of the opportunities afforded despite blackout conditions, Fire Guard duties, Home Guard parades, and the many calls on one's time consequent on war conditions. Other classes would be started as demands arise.'

For obvious reasons there was not a formal opening meeting.

'The coffee- and serving-rooms continue open until 10 p.m., and, on Friday evenings in particular, there is generally a numerous gathering. Our Superintendent, D. M. C. Gill, is always available and approachable in the coffee-room, except on those occasions when he is adding to his many accomplishments by the study and practice of drawing and painting. Mr and Mrs Pont, with little or no assistance, are carrying on magnificently, and spare no time nor thought in preparing meals for members and visitors, including members of outside bodies. How they keep the College in generally such good condition passeth man's comprehension.

'The Executive Committee, Studies Committee and College Corporation continue their good work, and grudge no time from their restricted leisure, in order to safeguard and further the interests of the College.'

At this meeting 'Feingold was asked to move his seven

THE COUNCIL AND EMERGENCY COMMITTEE

resolutions advocating reconstruction of the Council . . . he spoke with evident sincerity, for half an hour taking each point in turn. . . . The Principal congratulated him on the way he had presented his resolutions, but as no seconder to the motions was found, the Council proceeded to other business. The Bursar presented the accounts . . . he was happy to say that as from next year the annual income of the College would be increased by some £400 as a result of husbanding our expenditure. He then referred to the Playing Field, and Bankes's generosity and successful care of the funds there, adding that "the destruction of our equipment at Edgware was to be made good by the Middlesex County Council".'

Sir Frederick Maurice, seconding the resolution, said he was glad to hear that the Corporation had now paid for the whole of the new building. After various reports and College activities had been noted a letter was read moving that the Council give favourable consideration to reducing the age of admittance to the College from 16 to 14.

The Executive Committee undertook to inquire into this possibility in its general survey of future plans. To reassure those who might be alarmed at this – it may be stated here that this brain child of Bowley's died an early and natural death!

'Thanks to the leniency of the Paper Control,' the *Journal* comments, 'we are enabled to publish this *Journal*, which we are sure is welcome not only amongst members serving abroad, but amongst those at home unable to get to the College. To those who have anything interesting to relate an invitation is extended.'

Council Meetings, January 1944
'. . . The meetings were unusual in that they were devoted solely to the discussion of the Executive Committee's Report on the Future of the College which had been prepared by the Vice-Principal.

'. . . The recommendations aim at eradicating any weaknesses in organization which may in the past have existed, and fitting the College to face the changed conditions with which it will meet in the period after the war.

'So far, all the proposals made are tentative and subject to revision. . . . The Executive Committee has been considering the matter of its report for some months and has had the advantage of the expert advice of Professor Keeton of London University, of Mr Savage, Education Officer of the London County Council, and of Canon Spencer Leeson, Headmaster of Winchester.

'... The recommendations of the Report on the subject of the classes to be held after the war are very detailed and were favourably received by the Council. There were to be talks and lectures within the College after classes by distinguished specialists in their subjects.

'... Briefly ... they may prove to be of two types, one which will make a popular appeal and another which will concern itself with a particular subject studied at the College. It is likely that certain of them will take place during the week when classes have finished for the evening.

'It is recommended that much more care be given to the enrolment of new students. Each should be interviewed and advised as to a suitable course of study. He should not undertake too many subjects, nor should these be unrelated without good reason.

'There is much to be done to see that adequate use is made of the Library. Plans were under discussion for the day-time use of the College by the Board of Education as a training college for teachers.'

May 1944

'On May 24th, the Council gave final consideration to the Report on the Future of the College. There was a good attendance in spite of the exacting calls upon the members of 'total war'. Lord Greene conducted the proceedings with that quiet effectiveness that characterizes all he does ... warm thanks were expressed to Frank Gahan and his wife for drafting and preparing the report.

'Owing to the heavy calls on his time as Master of the Rolls, Lord Greene was forced to resign the Principalship. He moved that Sir Wilfrid Eady – who was not unfamiliar with the college, having taught there – be elected in his place. Sir Wilfrid had a very distinguished career in the Civil Service, was greatly interested in education and was prepared to devote his abilities to the College. The Bursar seconded the motion.'

'*Classes*. During the past session (1943–4) there have been 13 classes; 2 in English, 1 in citizenship, 1 in French, 2 in

German, 2 in Russian, 1 in Geography, 2 in mathematics, 1 in art, and 1 in English literature.

'Recently Barrett has succeeded in reviving the orchestra with an enrolment of twelve. The Art Class held an exhibition last August and is to hold another next July.

'. . . Meanwhile an attempt has been made to interest all members of the College serving in H.M. Forces, who can afford the time, in an essay scheme under which they are invited to record their experiences or express their views on some selected topic. . . . "Gifts of books" were to be given to the "more meritorious essays",' and, 'it is hoped that some of the essays . . . will be suitable for publication in the *Journal*.'

In fact, though a few essays were received, the response to this invitation was poor, the exigencies of service life not being conducive to essay writing. But two men, L.A.C. N. Penfold, and Corporal P. Norris, both of the R.A.F. Mediterranean Expeditionary Force sent essays that were judged 'worthy of recognition' and each was sent a book 'to mark the appreciation the College feels for those who undertake so serious a task under difficult conditions'.

Council Meeting, June 27th, 1944
College Buildings.

'The University Tutorial College is now in occupation during the day-time of fifteen rooms in the college. Their tenancy is in every way satisfactory, and the most cordial relations exist between them and the college. Their tenancy will end shortly after hostilities cease, and the Emergency Committee has been considering the possibility of the College thereafter being used in the day-time as a teachers' training college under the Board of Education. If satisfied that such a use would not prejudice the College's normal activities, the Emergency Committee proposes to ask Corporation to negotiate a lease to the Board of Education. It appears to the Committee that it would be a great advantage to the College to have teachers who will be going to schools all over London acquainted with the work of the College and the facilities it offers to adult students. Eleven rooms in the College are still occupied by the Zone Headquarters of the Home Guard.

'Council has just published its Report on "The Future of the

College". Copies of this have been sent to all *Journal* subscribers, members serving in H.M. Forces and other College members whose addresses are available.'

At the Council Meeting in July 1945

'The Principal suggested that he be empowered to send a letter of welcome in the name of the Council to returning serving members. This proposal was warmly supported . . . and unanimously agreed to.' (Unhappily the letter was not printed and thus has faded into oblivion.)

'The Principal then moved that time spent by College members in H.M. Forces should count as continued membership . . . not to count towards an old students' qualification . . . but to enable them to take part in elections to Council on their return.

'The Bursar then introduced the accounts . . . and drew attention to the steady increase in expenditure due to the building up of the staff in anticipation of more normal times. A study of the forecast of expenditure for a normal year would show that the College must depend on a day-time letting of some part of the building for some years to come . . . we should avoid dependence on a grant from the Ministry of Education as far as possible . . . and try to continue on the present lines until our centenary in 1954, when some form of appeal might be a possibility. . . . The question of war damage repairs still presented difficulties. In the electrical installations there was much to be done before they could be considered satisfactory. Thus as the war ended, new problems rose in the College. They continue up to the present time. Certain remarks made at the Old Students' Supper by the guest of honour, the Right Honourable Herbert Morrison, in this first year of peace, are so apt to the situation, it seems worth while to quote them here for they summarize much of what is finest in the College tradition. He said, "I see the College as a shining example of voluntary association for a purpose. I see in its common-room, the heart of the College, the sense of free, corporate fellowship where all men enter as equal persons. . . . I see also in the College the spirit of true democracy which makes its own rules and controls its own organization. Keep that light burning. Keep the vitality of the College, by each taking your share of its tasks – your share of responsibility. . . .'

XXVI

WAR EMERGENCY COMMITTEE REPORT

Copies of this Report were sent to all members serving in H.M. Forces and to other College members whose addresses were available.

THE chronicle of the College in the Second World War comes fittingly to a close with an account of its crowning achievement, the publication of the Report of the War Emergency Committee, and in a lighter vein, the 'Thank You Concert' organized by the students.

The Report is a long document. Only extracts can be quoted here giving the reader some idea of the aims and hopes that form its background.

Emergency Committee. Extracts from its Report, 1944

Introductory – 'During the war the College for the first time in its history has ceased to function in any real sense as a College. This . . . gives it a remarkable opportunity for planning on future ideal lines. Council has considered the future *without regarding itself as tied to any preconceived ideas*. Its Executive has . . . consulted outside experts . . . notably Mr Savage, Education Officer of the London County Council, former senior Chief Inspector of the Board of Education; Canon Spencer Leeson, headmaster of Winchester, and Professor Keaton of London

University. Fortunately the organization of the College places it in an exceptionally favourable position for experiment, and the break which has occurred ... has enabled the educational and administrative problems to be considered in a manner that ought to ensure ... that its sound future policy will not be prejudiced by the reintroduction of features that in the past have lowered the College standard, or diverted its activities from its main aim of providing a liberal education ...'

Number of students – 'It is desirable to limit the number of students from the moment the College restarts. Experience after the last war showed that the value of the College was to be measured not by the number of students enrolled, but by the quality of the education it gave ... the ideal number of students is about 800, with some latitude to ensure that men ... returning from the services or other wartime services are not shut out ...'

Age of students – 'The age at which students are admitted should not be lowered ... it is next to impossible to mix youths of 15 or 16 with much older men with any hope of securing real corporate unity ...'

Classes to be offered – 'In spite of greatly increased facilities offered elsewhere for adult education, the College remains unique in being a College for men only, which puts its main emphasis on being a place of corporate learning where education is not confined to instruction, but consists in the maintenance of a proper balance between study, athletics, the intellectual life of the common-room and learned Societies, and the social life of the College ... the College should maintain its policy of refusing to teach purely vocational subjects ... to draw the line is difficult, however ... (here the report elaborates and gives examples) ... those in charge will have constantly in their minds the spiritual, intellectual and social aims of the College. ... The attitude of the student towards his studies, and life in the College is probably of more importance than the subject he studies ...'

Boards of study – 'For each group of studies there will be a board which will direct the work into the right channels, ensure a proper standard of teaching, and ensure that the policy of that group is reviewed in the light of the *very best expert advice*. The Chairman will in each case be a distinguished educationalist . . . specially interested in the subject, and in securing as voluntary teachers, men not only with the necessary competence . . . but the *spiritual and intellectual qualities* which would fit them to take a place in the general College life. . . . To co-ordinate the work of the boards a Dean of Studies or similar official will be appointed . . . the studies committee will not be revived . . . experience showed that members concerned themselves almost exclusively with matters affecting their own groups. . . . Members of the boards would be full members of the College . . . and the more brilliant teachers no longer able to spare sufficient time for teaching, could continue to serve in an advisory capacity . . .'

Lectures by distinguished visitors – 'The pre-war Saturday lectures by famous men had long had to be abandoned . . . it would however be of greatest benefit to have frequent visits from men of recognized authority on matters of general interest. Of late years there has been an appalling tendency for the ordinary man to express emphatic views, and agitate for particular policies . . . in profound ignorance of the factors to be considered . . . distinguished men will be invited to . . . speak on their special subjects . . . at 9 p.m. (after classes). All talks will be informal with ample opportunity for asking questions, all students will be encouraged to regard attendance as a valuable part of their education . . .'

Enrolment – 'The problem of what class a student should take is a very serious one and ought to be dealt with with great care . . . each student should be interviewed by someone competent to give him disinterested advice . . .'

Teachers – 'A sound long term policy . . . depends on establishing an effective contact with universities and public schools. Prospective teachers cannot become interested in the College at too early an age. . . . In the teaching of languages it ought to be possible to enlist the help of embassy or consular officials to obtain, at any rate for the purposes of supervision, the help of native teachers . . .'

Contact with outside bodies – 'The work of the College would benefit very greatly by developing contacts with outside bodies. For some years before the war the holiday club arranged holidays abroad for members of the College that were an unqualified success. There is no reason why the College . . . should not establish valuable relations with bodies abroad that are interested in adult education . . . and why members of the College should not see something of the work done in adult education in other countries. . . . The same principle should be applied in this country, and an effort made to make the College the natural meeting place for those interested in adult education and in sound educational experiment. . . . The local connections of the College also are of great importance . . . steps should be taken to call the attention of the responsible railway officials at St Pancras to the advantages the College offers to the railway men of the district.'

XXVII

OLD STUDENTS' CLUB ANNUAL FUNCTIONS—1939-45

IN the following pages the reader will find accounts of the Old Students' Club annual luncheons, or suppers, in the war period 1939-45.

They are collected together in one chapter not only because in this form they present a clearer picture, but because, scattered through the book among other items, they seem irrelevant and would tend to break the continuity of the story it sets out to tell.

Old Students' Club 63rd Annual Supper, 1939

The wheel has turned full circle. Once again, as in the First World War, the Old Students' Supper has become a luncheon.

'A special wartime luncheon was held in the common-room on Sunday, December 10th.' The number of guests present was fifty, the limited number for which it was possible to cater at that time; 'a small but friendly gathering to keep the event alive', as the acting Chairman (Torrington) of the Club described it. . . . 'Thirty-six members of the College are serving with His Majesty's Forces and the Speaker had heard that to print a list of those on National Service would take two whole issues of the *Journal.*' Reference was made earlier in the speech to 'difficulties in connection with the proper use of the science laboratories. The Bursar (Ellis Franklin) and H. M. Clarke, Chairman of the Studies Committee, had begun to prepare a scheme. . . . A committee, of which Sir A. Seward had consented to become Chairman, had been set up . . . and plans were completed so that the science studies in the College would attain a standard worthy of the laboratories we have here. The war had brought deferment . . . but the foundation had been laid, and the work of the Bursar and those associated with him would bear most useful fruit.'

Old Students' Luncheon, December 28th, 1940

It was reported at this luncheon that C. H. Perry had succeeded Alexander Hepburn as secretary of the Club Hepburn, a large granite-like Scot, had been a notable College man in his day – and especially active in working for the Furnivall Treats. 'This year has been exceptional,' said Bankes, but 'at any rate until the end of March 1940 it was more normal than any of us had a right to expect . . . (there had been) 286 class enrolments and some twenty classes were held . . .' Bankes referred to the only two known losses in the war – 'The late Principal, Sir Arnold Wilson, at first posted as missing, was now known to have been killed while serving as tail gunner in the R.A.F., and Daniel Knowlton – who had come to the College by way of the afternoon classes for unemployed men – had been killed while on active service in France. Knowlton's technical ingenuity and skill – he had faultlessly constructed a microscope by hand while attending these afternoon classes – had attracted the attention of his teacher and won him a place in the evening classes. Later he was employed by the College as a laboratory technician. Having a fine physique, he had on several occasions posed as a model for the Art Class. He and his friend had taken charge of the weedy flower-beds in front of the College and transformed them into small flower gardens. . . . He was the first of his unit to come forward when volunteers for France were called for.' A man of considerable potentiality and a devoted member of the College, his early death was a tragedy. Bankes then spoke of the future, reminding his audience that 'We are already making our plans for the time after the war is over – about subjects to be taught and our whole method of teaching. We shall want all the help we can get, and everyone who can to bring this College to the knowledge of his friends. We shall keep in touch with you and whatever happens the College will go on.'

Old Students' Club Luncheon, Saturday, December 27th, 1941, held at Lysbeth Hall, Soho Square

Remarking on the [recent bomb] damage to the College, the President, George Bankes, said that 'we owed a debt of gratitude to Ellis Franklin, the Bursar, who with the assistance of our architect had managed to get the place into some considerable order. We ought also to be grateful for the caretaker, Pont, who, during the month or so after Chapman left, had the full responsibility of looking after the College. He is a man of great determination and great qualities. All of us felt great confidence in his judgement . . .'

Note appearing in the February–March 1942 Journal *(but written December 1941)*

'This year the Old Students' Club invited me to the College Christmas luncheon (at Lysbeth Hall), a very gracious gesture which I deeply appreciated. I trust the editor (of the *Journal*) may spare me a fraction of space in which to express my thanks to those who dared for me this break with a long tradition . . . to me it was a singularly happy experience. M. Franklin.'*

Report in the Journal *of Old Students' Club Luncheon, January 15th, 1943 (1942 Luncheon)*

There was a record wartime gathering, and the reception in the coffee-room prior to the luncheon was the occasion of much renewing of old acquaintances. After the toast of the King, that was received 'with acclamation', the Chairman (Bankes) said 'once again our thoughts would be about members of the College who were not able to be present because they were serving their country in different parts of the world.' The speaker then referred to Reid and Ron Badger, both in the R.A.F., and both of whom had lost their lives while on active service, owing to tragic accidents. . . . Bankes also spoke of the organizers of the luncheon, 'in particular C. H. Perry who had been a member of the College for fifty-one years . . . and assisted

* I was, of course invited as representing the Ladies' War Work Party.

by his admirable wife had managed to keep the Old Students' Club in being during the most difficult years of its existence'. Referring to the events of the year, the speaker said the College classes had revived to a limited extent ... The activities on the Playing Field had been reduced, but thanks largely to the efforts of Allsop, the Bowls Club had been kept alive. ... Dick Ramage and Bill Walder (home after serious wounds, from North Africa) have returned to the Cricket Club.

'A. S. Lupton had retired from the Presidency of the Old Students' Club and gone to live in Kendal. For more than 40 years a member of the College, he had been Vice-Principal and also teacher.

'Regarding his (Bankes's) election to the post of President, O.S.C., he had consented on two conditions – first that the Committee should make sure that Randall (who had given long years of valuable service to the College) was unwilling to stand; and that after the war the Club should be free to choose any one they liked in his (Bankes's) place.' Bankes referred to the difficulties there had been in trying to get on without a superintendent after C. Chapman left, in 1942. "We were very glad," he said, "that D. M. C. Gill, who knew about administration and education and had taught at the College before the war, was able to take the post." Speaking of losses from death, change of domicile and other causes, sustained by the College in 1942, Bankes referred to Isaake (custodian of the commonroom), Julius Jacob (brother of Lionel Jacob) and to "Lady Maurice, who, while her husband was Principal, supported him in all his work for the College and won golden opinions for her friendliness to members, and for the interest she maintained in all aspects of its work."'

F. Gahan (Vice-Principal), responding, said: 'When we go to seek teachers and officers to administer our affairs, we ought not to go humbly trying to persuade people to come to us, we ought to go proudly, because any person who comes within the College walls is going to get more than he gives. There is no source of advice that is not open to us, and already, chiefly through the activities of the Bursar, we are in touch with educational authorities who are going to advise us as to the best course for the future. With this and our voluntary system and amateur enthusiasm, we hope to attain to the efficiency of

OLD STUDENT'S CLUB FUNCTIONS

professionalism, preserving all the virtues that characterized the College in its early days. As to the future, we must seek a high standard in our teachers; we must insist on diligent work by our students, and their recognition of the necessity for discipline in learning.' The Vice-Principal then referred to College finances. 'A fund had been started to replace the capital and during the year the Bursar was able to inform us that the capital had been entirely replaced. The College was very grateful to all those who . . . had contributed to the replacement of the capital. But again, those who knew the Bursar knew that replacement was never enough, so he has started another fund that marks an important development in the College – a fund to create a capital which will enable us from time to time to have money available for up-to-date equipment, and the proper discharge in the most up-to-date manner of our educational responsibilities.'

Old Students' Club, January 1944

The annual luncheon took place on January 15th, in the common-room of the College. The President, George Bankes, was in the chair, and there were seventy-four present.

'An admirable luncheon, pre-war as to quality and quantity, was served, Mr and Mrs Pont excelling themselves.' As at the previous wartime luncheon in the College stewarding and help in the kitchen and serving-room were undertaken by the ladies of the Work Party. It was an extremely happy function, both for the guests in the common-room and those assisting Mr and Mrs Pont outside.

Among the letters from the Forces received after this function came one from Cpl. F. Kreeser, R.A.F. who was on leave and able to attend. He wrote, 'As you may well imagine I was very pleased to be able to go along to the O.S. Luncheon. This was the first I was able to attend since the war, and it did me good to be back again in the old familiar surroundings, and to meet old friends. . . . I have had a promotion since you saw me, which I hope will be my last one, for I am only hoping for the day when the *good efforts of the Work Party can be turned to other ways for the benefit of College men*.' Did he foresee the birth of the post-war Ladies Association?

OLD STUDENT'S CLUB FUNCTIONS

The Old Students' Club Supper, December 15th, 1945

Peace! And the Old Students' Club Supper has reverted to its old form, the luncheons that kept it alive during the war have become, happily, things of the past.

The only survival of that wartime organization is the voluntary serving staff. The Old Work Party, now the Ladies Association, continues the pleasant wartime tradition of voluntary service for this typical College occasion.

In 1939 the guest of honour at the Founders' Night celebrations was to have been the Right Hon. Herbert Morrison. But war intervened, flinging its menacing dark shadow across all normal life. The function that should have marked Founders' Night was cancelled.

With an artistry, conscious or unconscious, for the first of the resumed Old Students' Club Suppers in December 1945, the organizers contrived to produce, as their guest of honour for the evening, the Right Hon. Herbert Morrison.

Thus, as in so many other aspects of College life, the new order opened, linked closely with the old.

XXVIII

LETTERS FROM THE HOME FRONT–CIVIL AND MILITARY

All the letters printed in the following pages were, unless contrary information is given, written to Mrs Franklin, as representing the Work Party.

NO account of the years between 1940 and 1945 could give a true picture without a glance at the air attack that carried the war to the Home Front. McShee's experience is typical of so many, and for that reason it finds a place in this book. Until he joined the R.A.F. he gave loyal and ungrudging service to the College, regardless of personal tribulation. Briggs writes more briefly, with rather touching restraint, but his experience was no less harsh.

From an Old Student, E. C. Briggs, to Sweetman, November 1940.

'Just a line hoping you are keeping fit and have not been troubled by our friends' fireworks, as it leaves us fairly well. . . . I am sorry to say we were bombed, and I have lost everything, not a stick of furniture . . . all our clothes have gone, so when we start we shall have to buy a new home entirely . . . but that will not be till after the war, so I hope you will excuse me for not coming to the College, as travelling has been rotten lately . . .'

From London Civil Defence, L. E. McShee, undated, but probably 1942.

'I was the happiest College man to receive that parcel . . . that day I was bombed out with the house where I was born totally demolished . . . it left me with a headache for a week. There is no doubt that I was grateful to the W.M.C. Work Party for socks, for one difficulty was that I had only the one pair of socks! And the *six* nearly new pairs disappeared in the fire. I got out, how I could not tell you . . . I moved even quicker than Jack Robinson, and moaned with fear because I thought the house was falling on me and I would be trapped. I had previously been out putting out firebombs – three lots – and had gone in again for a few moments' thought and reflection. I wanted it, for it seemed this was one day when our number was up. We stayed on to put out another three lots of firebombs, and then decided to persuade everyone to get out of the street. They did not want much persuading. We insisted they did not go off to the Holborn Tube – if they had they would have been dead because people were killed at the moment on that spot. . . . Those people were eventually evacuated from the shelter we suggested they went to, so you can tell it was very hot, and 15 out of 20 houses went in Harpur Street. . . . The house was completely destroyed . . . only the two walls standing of the 200-year-old house where I was born, where my people had lived for 70 or 80 years. . . . Since that night all the houses have been demolished, so that I would not even recognize the street. . . . I had one of the best collections of Pitman books – all destroyed. I was grateful to so many students who had not returned the books I lent them! Thus I have something to recover after all. . . One young soldier put out more firebombs than I would want to see any man putting out on his own, but when we left off for a second because his mother had fainted, we had the whole street alight. . . . When the Badgers were bombed I thought how kind of the sick Mrs Franklin* to write to them. My happiness at the parcel and your kind letter exceeded theirs I think.'

Here is another different view of air raids.

From Gnr. W. Matt, A.A. Battery,† R.A., London, to the Work Party.

* I only had an attack of jaundice. M.F.
† This is the battery that was supplied with socks by the Work Party.

LETTERS FROM THE HOME FRONT

'The two books you sent me were quite a welcome surprise, and I read them, as you suggested, "between the raids". We were certainly having quite a lively time just then, and we were kept pretty busy, as you no doubt noticed. We contributed our full quota of the noise . . .'

Major Hugh M. Clark, one time College teacher and Chairman of the Studies Committee, writes to Ellis Franklin in 1941.

'We have moved about the country a lot lately. . . . We have plenty of operational tasks to carry out. I am still on the same job and not likely to get a regiment as long as this home defence goes on. However new methods of warfare, and changes in equipment to meet them make the job very interesting. I find myself with plenty of satisfactory and interesting jobs to do. Margaret [his wife] is still in the A.T.S. and with the infantry at Bedford. I see her most week-ends in town. . . . I have visited King's College, evacuated to Bristol, where they have not had such a peaceful time as they had hoped.* Whether they remain another session is problematic.

'My job takes me anywhere in the Eastern Command, and I have also a detachment of 80 men on Salisbury Plain, so when I get fed up with East Anglia I can evacuate myself to Wiltshire for a few days. The war seems to be going according to plan. That is, we keep on losing it until we get a win, and then it's over. At present the win is not in sight. I think about this time next year we ought to get a glimpse of it. Hope you have escaped air raid damage and that all the W.M.C. friends have done so also.

'I suppose the *Journal* has ceased.'

The last sentence is a statement, as he goes on to suggest an abbreviated circular of personal news to be sent to W.M.C. members. The statement was wrong, the *Journal* never ceased publication, but his war prophecies were much nearer the mark.

Physical Training Instructors can be Human

Sgt. B. Langdon. 'I am still trying to make men out of boys before their time – mere slips of boys, 17 and 18 years of age, are having to go through hard training to make them physically fit

---
* Bristol suffered heavy air raids, that destroyed its town centre.

for air-crew duties. I often wish that I was back in the College, taking all the men I knew so well.'

(Written by a former P.T. Instructor at the College.)

The last four letters in this group all come from the R.A.F. written to E. McShee – teacher of shorthand at the College.

P. Guymer, October 28th, 1940.
'This week my spirits have been suddenly revived and I have been bubbling over with enthusiasm . . . the fact is that one of your former and I hope, future shorthand pupils is at last able to make use of, for official purposes, the knowledge that you have formerly passed to him. . . . You can appreciate my delight after my Commanding Officer had told me to take my shorthand book with me whenever he calls for me. So at last they have discovered I can be of more use to them. We have some Polish airmen here and I am now only waiting to get the opportunity of teaching them English through French, and I shall indeed be happy. You see I am realizing now more than ever what the W.M.C. has done for me. . . . About a week ago I had my first trip in an aeroplane. It was a trip of 1 hour 40 minutes consisting of practice formation flying. The trip was not very exciting – not so thrilling as I thought it might be, but I felt very ill up there 6,000 feet nearer to heaven. When we came down I was looking forward to my next trip . . .

'I was in London again this week-end, but did not arrive until the air raid had commenced on Saturday evening.'

The letter below is typical of many received in the war years, particularly in its affection for the College, and concern for its future policy.

F/O G. Nichols, R.A.F., 1943.
'I can't hope to rival those members of the W.M.C. who have been holding the gorgeous East in fee and raising thirsts somewhere east or west of Suez. In fact my only achievement in the war so far is to have remained in the U.K. for over four years' service with the R.A.F. I have left Balloon Command and transferred to Bomber Command, and am gradually becoming acclimatized. . . . Once, in the summer of 1942, I made a

LETTERS FROM THE HOME FRONT

pilgrimage to the Sports Ground hoping to see Frank Lloyd & Co. in action between the wickets, but found their place usurped by a ladies' XI! Ichabod! Ichabod! It is reassuring to learn from the *Journal* that the College is still going strong and preparing for the important part it should play in any post-war educational scheme. The most prominent, and to my mind the most valuable characteristic of the College is that it is a microcosm of ideal democracy, where tolerance of the other man's viewpoint is the keynote. Tolerance is a very rare virtue these days. . . . How's the old College progressing now? . . . Education seems to be an important and vital part in shaping post-war happiness. . . . I presume the College is taking the necessary steps for setting in motion the machinery for adapting itself to new conditions and methods . . .'

From L.A.C. W. H. Richards (extracts from several letters).
'I am now L.A.C. and also, I have moved again. My new home is quite interesting. It is a mansion that once belonged to Empress Eugenie. With a slight stretch of the imagination one can quite imagine how lovely it must have been in its heyday.

'The stretch of imagination is required because the only furnishings are service beds, lockers, tables and chairs. . . . I have only just returned to my station from another course, this time a junior N.C.O.'s course lasting a month. I am very pleased to be back. . . . I find that I am very busy, life being just bed and work, except for thirty-six hours' leave once a fortnight.'

From L.A.C. Ron Badger, on a six months 'rest', acting as flying instructor in England after a long spell of foreign service.
'Thanks a lot for the May–June copy of the *Journal*. About a week previous to that I received a copy of the September–October issue. It had done quite a bit of travelling, but eventually caught me up. I wonder if there were any issues between these two? . . . Do you think I could get copies from you? I hope so. [The January–February issue was sent, and he must have received it a few days prior to his death.] I shall be due for fourteen days leave on August 4th, so hope to see you then. [The accident in which he lost his life occurred on August 4th.] I am fairly well settled in this part of Cumberland now. My job at present is flying instructor. I think I'm coping fairly well, but I

can't say I particularly care for it. I'd much rather be back in a squadron, even with the extra risks that might be involved. However, this so-called rest is only for six months, I hope, and then something might be done. I had a very enjoyable time on my tour of duty overseas, spending quite a little time in Canada, the States, and the West Indies. I think I saw all the West Indies from the air, and landed at quite a few islands. I loved every minute of it. . . . I wonder how much Cooks' Tours would have charged me for the trip in peace-time? I also visited South America, and by way of contrast, spent some time in the Arctic. All very interesting, and I wouldn't have missed any of it. England looked very beautiful on my arrival back in April, but if I have to go overseas again I shall not complain.'

This letter was written ten days before Ron Badger was killed in a flying accident in England, while taking a man on an instruction flight.

Hot Time in the Old Town
From the *Journal*. This account of an air-raid experience dated 29th December 1940 is unsigned. Such happenings were of almost nightly occurrence during the blitz. Neither the writer of this letter, nor McShee, are guilty of exaggeration.
'The alert moaned its hideous warning across London at 6.30. We noted the time and forgot all about it . . . about 7 o'clock the ack-ack were banging and thumping and barking. I was standing in the Teleprinter room. Pang! Something hit the steel shutters which cover the windows. Crash! exploded something immediately outside. Through the crack where the shutters joined I could see a vivid light and heard the swish, like the giant Christmas cracker, the Roman Candle. I raced into the Control Room yelling "Incendiary!"
'Grabbing bags of sand the engineers hared out of the building. . . . Like scalded cats we raced all ways at once dumping sand on the bombs. . . . Two of the engineers were already working like fiends smothering the bombs and fighting the fires which had started . . . but we could do nothing about the one right on top of the building, lodged inaccessibly between the chimneys . . . it was blazing fiercely . . . By this time many houses were on fire. . . . The fire engines arrived and were

immediately on the job. Efficiently and swiftly they had swung into action.

'The two men who had been smothering bombs suddenly reappeared. . . . They had done a good job . . . but from the grins on their faces you would think they had been up to some lark.

'The smoke had seeped into the building . . . tea was suggested to alleviate the wear and tear on our throats . . . I went to the Mess Room and got a bottle of milk . . . it was the only bottle and I thought we would have to go easy if we were to make it last till the morning. . . . I followed one of the engineers to the main hall. . . . The building rocked . . . I felt rather than heard the explosions. . . . In the terrifying darkness the place seemed to be collapsing on to me . . . I was in the middle of crashing chaos and black fury. I heard the shout, "Keep down!" but I was already down, thrown down. My tin hat had blown from my head, my glasses from my face. . . . Instinctively I clasped my head with my hands. Suddenly I became aware of something wet and sticky trickling down my face. . . . I thought, "I've stopped one." I could feel no pain. . . . I staggered to my feet and felt wetness trickling down the outside of my leg. My trousers were saturated. But still no pain. . . . I fumbled in the darkness. I found my spectacles and torch. I switched on the torch fully prepared to see my hands covered with blood, but to my astonishment the light revealed no sight of blood . . . only a colourless liquid. Something from the Battery Room, I thought, as I found myself outside that room, and its door had been blown in. I had no time to stop and think it out. The air was thick with dust. . . . In the hall I could hear someone coughing and retching. I guessed it to be one of the policemen – maybe he had been hurt. . . . By this time we had all got torches. . . .' The writer goes into considerable detail. . . . Miraculously the men in the place were safe, and the building had suffered only superficial damage, though 'the trouble,' as the account explains, 'had been caused by a high explosive and a land mine falling almost together. . . .

'The policeman I had heard,' the report continues, 'was suffering from shock, his colleague was taken away. He had been outside the building and had received the benefit of both the H.E. and the land mine. . . .

'We went to the Control Room and tried to clean things up.... The Senior sent two men over to the Emergency Control ... they started out for all the world like two schoolboys on a spree, to get across London through a rain of incendiaries....

'The maintenance engineer said the fires were closing in on us and if they weren't soon stopped we wouldn't be able to get through.

'The Senior decided to send the rest of the men over to the Emergency, keeping only one man back, and me....

'We settled down to try and make order out of chaos. Smoke-dried, we made tea, and I discovered that we had no milk. Then I remembered I had been carrying the bottle when the explosion hit me. What in the darkness I had imagined to be blood pouring down my face was – milk!'

The writer continues at some length to describe the horror of that night, the fires, fanned by a great wind – and the destruction – 'London,' he says, 'was on fire.... In the distance I could see the dome of St Paul's in an inferno of flame and smoke ... the Monument stood silhouetted against a sheet of flame.... Built to commemorate the Fire of London it certainly had a ring-side seat at this one.... We covered everything we could with sand.... It was the Devil's Carnival ...

'At last the firelight died down as the houses were gutted and the fires put out.... And in the morning I stood at the door and watched men going to work, threading their way through the wreckage ...

'As the dawn came everything was covered in a grey reddish haze, through which the figures stumbled.

'Wearily the dawn dragged into day ... the smoky mists rolled slowly away, and revealed pitiful desolation.'

XXIX

LETTERS FROM THE ROYAL NAVY

THESE letters from College men who served in the Royal Navy are arranged according to the men who wrote them, rather than chronologically. It is hoped that this manner of presenting them may help to give them some sort of coherence.

From Ord. Signalman C. T. Turner, October 1940.
'Whilst we are in training here as sailors, they seem to think it desirable to make us infantrymen at the same time. If you have ever tried doing funeral firing-party drill with a rifle that seems to be several degrees below zero, in the dim light of 6.30 a.m., you will know how the hands feel (or rather they don't feel at all). One can't handle a rifle with gloves on, so mittens would be most welcome . . .

'The life is not at all bad on the whole in this training camp, and we've a pretty decent set of chaps here of all types and tongues – it sounds like the tower of Babel at times. Like the College the Navy is a great leveller and you get B.Sc's and factory hands chumming together . . .'

From Sig. D. Turner, R.N. (January).
'I was very pleased to receive the *Journal*. . . . It is now almost a year since we breathed good English air, during which time we have done quite a lot of globe-trotting and are still imitating the Wandering Jew! I'm still on the same little ship, almost two years aboard her . . . books are always welcome and will be

gladly received. . . . I wish I could write something of interest about places visited, but afraid that is forbidden. . . . Have you by any chance a largish street map of London that we could stick up on our mess-deck walls please? It would be a centre of interest for hours – not only to us homesick Londoners, but we could educate those who have never been there.' [The map was duly dispatched.]

From J. Boyce.
'My job is a wireless operator on the rescue launches. We usually operate . . . when any of our aircraft make forced landings in the sea. It is an interesting job, and I get a great kick out of it. The boys here are a grand lot, like the lads at the College.'

From W. L. Lovejoy, Seaman R.N., 1942.
'Just a few lines to let you know I am once more a survivor, fortunately getting away without any injuries. I am now on a battleship, which I find a little larger than the two previous ships. I hope the College is carrying on despite the circumstances, and I am certainly *still* looking forward to the time when we shall all be back and business is "as usual". . . . Please give my best wishes to all at the College, and all those on active service.'

From W. L. Lovejoy, A.B., 1943.
'Very many thanks for your letter and College *Journal*. I was very glad to hear that the College is carrying on, despite the difficulties of the age, and I am quite sure that after the war the College will be more popular than ever before. We had forty-eight hours survivors' leave when the *Naiad** went down, so I took the opportunity of seeing Cairo. It is a pity I could not have seen Pat Guymer, who used to work with me at the Town Hall. . . . I was fortunate to get some leave somewhere in Africa, where among many other things we visited a native chieftain in his kraal. It was in a temperate zone of Africa and there was some of the most beautiful countryside I have ever seen. We are now able to get tea, coconuts, and all sorts of tropical fruits at abnormally cheap prices.'

* It would seem that Lovejoy had the doubtful pleasure of multiple experience as a survivor from torpedoed ships.

LETTERS FROM THE ROYAL NAVY

From Leading Stoker J. Harvey, December.

'I was drafted to a corvette, the duties of which, as you probably know, consists of convoy work. Thus I was able to visit Newfoundland. It was winter-time, and as there had been a heavy fall of snow, the port of call had a Christmas card aspect. There were no black-out restrictions and consequently one was able to walk around during the hours of darkness without fear of running foul of obstacles and pedestrians. The shop windows had a fine display of goods – coupon free – but owing to the duty and rate of exchange, prices were high ... fishing ... has been curtailed owing to part of the fishing fleet being taken over for war duties. The majority of the fisher folk are also in the Forces, many of them serving in the Royal Navy. Most of the buildings are entirely of wood; wood being used because it is easy to obtain and cheaper than importing bricks and stone. . . . The town – if it can be called such – has a neglected appearance, as if it had been left for a generation, and then reoccupied. The only reminder we had of home was the football pitch, used quite a lot by the Navy. There was not a blade of grass on it – what a comparison with the College football pitch!'

From E. V. Harris, AB/WK, R.N., 1943.

'Very many thanks for your letter . . . the above address is more or less a drafting depot. After completing a job on a ship or station one is returned here to await draft to somewhere – heaven knows where; but one just hopes for the best. Whilst waiting, work is found and a daily job is given. . . . My particular job is P.O.'s messman, polishing mess deck, laying tables, washing dishes, etc.; serving meals at meal-times, is just one glorious rush. As far as jobs go it is not bad, but I don't think I would take it up as a means of livelihood when I return to civvy street. . . . I am very pleased to hear that the M.C.C.* finished up strongly, and wish them every success in 1944, when, God willing, I hope we shall all be returned to our homes.'

L. J. Gill appears to have served on a number of different ships as these letters show.

From L. J. Gill, R.N. H.M.S., *Franklin*.

'You will see that I am attached to a ship of your own

* Maurice Cricket Club.

name. . . . She was named after the doughty admiral of the late eighteenth century of that name. . . . Like others of the same name the old boy was apparently helped considerably by the interest shown in his work or his hobbies by his wives. No, although he was a sailor, I don't think he was a polygamist, but he had two wives. Anyway, it is a very happy ship, and I consider myself lucky in being attached to her, although it is probably only for a very short time.'

From L/Wrtr. L. Gill, R.N.
'I have left the old ship (H.M.S. *Bellona*), but not before I had the experience of being in action with her. At one time I was working very hard for fifteen or sixteen hours a day, and often wondered if it was going to be worth it, then came D-day, and now you know the result, and it really was worth it. The last twelve months have been a most interesting time from an operational point of view, and now that I am still safe I can look back and say that I would not have missed it for worlds.'

From L/Radio Mechanic A. Hitchcock, R.N.
'Many thanks for the copies of the *Journal*. . . . I have been knocking around in some pretty lonely places, Iceland and Archangel mainly, so got out of touch with things a bit. I have just recently, however, spent three months in the College of Technology in — on a radio course, which helped me to get into the swing of things again. I have not come into contact with any old College friends during my travels, but I did hear from a member of the old Spanish class, who is serving as a photographer in the S. African Air Force, and, looking through the *Journal*, there were letters from some of my friends . . .

'At the moment I'm waiting in barracks for a ship. I expect to go any day now. . . . I would be most grateful for any spare books you may have, the last lot you sent me were well read by me and my shipmates, and they eventually joined the library of one of H.M. corvettes, and the comforts sent with them are still giving good service after two years.'

From Pte. W. J. Harvey, H.M. Hospital Ship.
'Please convey my heartiest thanks to members of the Work Party. . . . England seems far away at the moment, but to

receive parcels like this makes it a little nearer. The war seems to drag on, but one day it will be over, and once more we will be able to fraternize in the Common-Room again. I have to put that in capitals for I think the common-room symbolizes the College. Men from all walks of life in comradeship – I can't imagine it ever dying, no one who has once experienced the atmosphere of the College will ever forget it, or want to part with it.'

The following two letters describe two sorties of the famous Malta convoys. They are long, but vividly written, and give a striking picture of what was involved. It seems worth while to include them, almost unabridged. The writer, in his normal life, is an ordinary, everyday, agreeable person; a bachelor, he lived with his mother – his chief interest is music, his instrument, the fiddle; his hobby, collecting gramophone records. Not what the imagination pictures as a 'heroic figure'. But of such stuff, as these letters plainly show, are heroes made.

An Exciting Naval Experience. S/Lt. J. A. Clements, R.N.V.R.*

'The most exciting experience for nearly every naval man must surely be his first experience of war at sea. It certainly was for me!

'The noise of falling and bursting bombs, and the damage they cause, was not new to me, having lived through the worst of the London "blitz" and performed the fire-watching duties which were then so essential, but it was the first time that I had formed a part of something which was itself the sole target.

'A feeling of excitement began to grow at that Scottish port at which, after we had ammunitioned ship for a day and a night, and loaded the decks and every conceivable space with torpedo bodies, torpedo war-heads, aeroplane tyres and parts, and crates of various sizes, the captain told us we were to rush badly needed goods to Malta. They were so badly needed in fact, that we were going to take the most direct route – that through the Mediterranean from Gibraltar – and would be the first ship that had attempted that route for some time, the others having gone via the Cape. He was proud of that. We were going to "bust our way through" and he was confident of success. He

* 'The exciting experience' occurred while Clements was still a rating.

said that we could look upon it as a Mediterranean cruise – one for which, in peace time, people paid hundreds of pounds.

'The first part of this cruise was uneventful, but excitement increased as we neared the Rock. We had been timed to arrive at night, and an oiler was then expected alongside. So that the oiler's crew, and possibly fifth columnists, should not know that a new ship had arrived in the Mediterranean, we were ordered to wear our white caps, and, if necessary, give as our own the name of another ship of the same class which had been stationed there for some time. All went well, however, and we left while it was still dark with the destroyer F— in company.

'We spotted an enemy reconnaissance plane from time to time and were anxious to shoot it down, but it took care never to come within range of the close-range weapons, and the gunnery officer would not permit us to fire the H.A. guns owing to a desire to conserve ammunition. A Catalina flying-boat also appeared at infrequent intervals, but after circling the ship two or three times on each occasion, eventually disappeared and was not seen again.

'Excitement rose high as we neared the Straits of Pantellaria. That is the most dangerous part of any trip between Gibraltar and Malta, because of the enemy's E-boat base so very few miles away.

'Our speed had been arranged so that we passed through the Straits at night, but for safety's sake we were closed up at action stations all night long. The crew of the after tower, or director (of which I was one), took it in turn to supplement the bridge and other look-outs by keeping watch with the aid of the control officer's glasses, and the air defence officer took care to ensure that we remained awake and alert by calling us through his telephone from time to time and exhorting us to keep a particularly good look-out for the speedy enemy E-boats. We became very tired and cramped closed up in a confined space for so long, and doubtless those in the turrets, magazines, and other parts of the ship did too, but at long last light appeared in the eastern sky, the sun came over the horizon, and we were safely through. A reconnaissance plane still shadowed us though, so we expected things to happen sooner or later, and they did.

'The destroyer F— had been hard put to it to keep up with us, and when only a few miles from Malta she suddenly heeled an astonishing number of degrees to starboard – so many that it seemed she would not be able to right herself. I drew the attention of the director's crew to this incident, and we were most relieved when, after several minutes had passed, she succeeded in righting herself again. This incident, however, had caused her to ship the sea down her funnels. The sea had also washed one of her boats away. I learned afterwards that her rudder had jammed, and as she was consequently in difficulties her C.O. requested us to pick up her boat. The ship had just turned to attempt this when we were surprised by the sudden firing of our port pom-poms and other close-range weapons. The after group of 525's (then controlled from the after tower), upon instructions from the bridge, were trained upon a solitary enemy plane away on the starboard quarter, so upon the instructions of the director control officer (a smart little captain of marines) I opened the rear windscreen to see what was happening. I was just in time to see a large bomb enter the water a few feet away, and the huge shower of water thrown up by another further for'ard. I looked up and saw a number of German bombers circling and diving towards the ship. In the port waist a wooden crate containing a torpedo war-head was blazing furiously. Reporting all this, I quickly shut the windscreen with one hand and grabbed my tin hat with the other, but before I was able to sit down again, I felt a terrific smack in my left thigh – as though I had been hit with great force by a cricket ball. It nearly knocked me down. I felt the sting of the impact and the blood running down my leg, and I sat down on my uncomfortable little seat with my injured leg stretched out over the small iron door in the deck which gave access to the director. It felt easier that way.

'I was annoyed at having been hit so early in the action, and decided to say nothing about it until the fighting was over. My leg began to feel stiff and heavy, but did not seem to bleed so much when stretched out straight.

'The following fifteen minutes or so were tremendously exciting. The range-taker lost his nerve and, becoming hysterical, pointed to the sky and screamed: "There they are, look. Up there! Up there! Three, four, five of them; dozens of them. Look, up there!" But the control officer calmly patted his head and said: "All right, laddie, keep calm, keep calm."

'Then came a time when the guns of X turret were trained right on the director, and someone shouted: "My God! Look at X turret. They'll blow us to pieces. Tell them to train round quickly." It seemed an age before I received their reply on my telephone and saw them train on another bearing.

'Yes. It was undoubtedly very exciting, and I should probably have seen the action all through from the director had not another of the crew received a bomb splinter in his right forearm, and the control officer, in trying to open the door to let him out, told me to move my foot and gave it a kick to speed the movement. My exclamation and reply of "Oh! Please don't do that," to a second kick (through being unable to move it quickly enough the first time) let the cat out of the bag. He ignored my request to stay and protestations that I could carry on, and insisted upon my going below with the other rating for treatment. As a result, my last duty in that action was to request the bridge to send two reliefs to the after tower.

'It was disappointing having to go below at that stage, but I found it still exciting, when, having had my wounds temporarily dressed by the Padre (I prevented him from cutting up my clothes I remember) and received an injection of morphia, I lay on a stretcher in the comparative safety of the captain's cabin, and listened in a semi-conscious and delightfully lazy state to the continued firing of the ship's guns and the whistling of the bombs as they gathered momentum and tore through the air to straddle the ship in an ever-increasing circle . . . and then at last silence – or what seemed silence after so much noise. The battle was over. A little later we entered the Grand Harbour at Malta. We had succeeded in "busting our way through".

'Most of the serious injuries among the ship's crew were caused by a bomb that exploded in the air abreast the port pom-pom. In addition, it killed eleven, including the captain's secretary, the master-at-arms, and the gunner's mate.

'It is a piece of that same bomb (after extraction from my femur at the second attempt) that I now have as a souvenir. I was lucky.

'In company with the more seriously wounded I was carried off the ship on a stretcher. . . . A short ambulance ride and I was taken out and carried past groups of sympathetic Maltese faces down the entire length of one of Malta's now famous rock shelters, to a first-aid dressing room at the far end. There my wounds received another dressing and I was carried out again to the still waiting ambulance.

'On the way to the hospital (in Malta) I learned from a fellow casualty (he had been gassed in "A" magazine) that the ship had received a direct hit on the fo'c'sle and that the bomb had gone right through the ship (missing the for'ard magazine by inches) and out at the bottom without exploding. What amazing luck! And what an experience! I wouldn't have missed it for anything, for apart from the excitement of engaging the enemy I have discovered that being wounded in action is not necessarily so terrible as people imagine, and that I have thereby gained an added confidence for the future.'

Malta Convoy by A.S. J. A. Clements
'The time is mid-morning and harbour routine is in full swing. The Red Watch are in good spirits, it is the day for their afternoon's leave ashore. But soon the atmosphere changes. Excitement abounds. Orders for the routine at sea have suddenly appeared on the notice-board, and inform us that we will "slip" in the early evening.

'Conjecture is rife. . . . We are going home; but that is not very likely. We are going to bombard the coast at such a place. We are to take a convoy to another. But the lower deck do not know, at any rate at this stage, where we are going.

'There is a great activity everywhere preparing the ship for sea. Everything movable is lashed and made fast. The anchors are weighed and the ship leaves her berth. Another adventure has begun. Some of the Red Watch wonder if they will ever go go ashore again.

'The men go to their defence stations, a couple of hours pass. Ah, the captain will speak over the ship's broadcasting system in five minutes. He tells us that we are to form part of another convoy which is taking much needed goods to a certain small, but very badly blitzed, island [Malta].

'The sun sets, and we close up at Dusk Action Stations. From my position aloft I see all the merchant ships surrounded and interspersed by the ships of H.M. Navy. It is an impressive sight.

'The first night is uneventful, but the morning brings Action Stations, and we know that this time it means business.

'Everyone has a job to do, and needs to do it thoroughly as the enemy makes his presence known. Fifteen bombers suddenly appear and dive on the convoy. The air is torn by terrific bursts of gunfire as we fight for our lives. Some can feel the heat of the gun flashes upon their faces. The naval ships increase speed and slew first to port then to starboard, to avoid the falling bombs. One has a near miss as a huge bomb falls a few feet from her bows. An unfortunate merchantman – a tanker – receives a direct hit and is greedily swallowed by the rapacious waves. At the same time a calm voice comes through the loud speakers. It is the gunnery officer speaking from the bridge. "A Junkers is about to pass right over the ship. Get it." It passes over. The close range weapons give it all they've got, and it flies on with smoke streaming from its tail, while the other ships help it on its way when within reach of their guns.

'The enemy's planes are driven off, and we breathe freely again, but it is not long before they return and continue their attack with renewed vigour. Opportunity is taken of another lull to leave our action stations and dash off for some food. But before we can get it the guns are firing and the bombs are falling again, so back we go to our posts at full speed. And so it goes on the whole day long.

'At last the sun begins to set in a blaze of golden light. "Keep a good look-out for torpedo bombers and E boats," is the cry. The barrage is intensified as yet more bombers dive out of the sun. The noise is deafening, the shell-bursts and tracers make red and yellow patterns in the sky. But still they come. Six of them make a concentrated attack upon a destroyer. Bombs fall upon and around her, she hasn't a chance, but blows up with a burst of flame, and a tremendous cloud of smoke arises and hangs in the air for many minutes. It seems impossible that there can be any survivors.

'The ships are still silhouetted against the slowly fading light, and we long for complete darkness after such a day.

'At long last the light has gone and the night is upon us, but that does not mean a good sleep. There are always the U-boats, and the men must keep watch throughout the night.

'There is an early dawn. Quite soon the sun shines brightly

from a blue sky upon a blue sea. The heat is intense. We look at the convoy, it steams peacefully along. Yesterday's battle might have been a terrifying nightmare, but for the fact that we still feel tired and another glance at the convoy shows us that two ships are missing.

'For tactical reasons we have altered course in the night and now ride through a patch of sea discoloured, greasy and dirty looking. It is the spot at which the tanker was sunk, and the surface of the sea is covered with oil.

'Today is similar to yesterday. We are not left alone for long. Aircraft, guns, bombs and more bombs. In turning sharply to port to avoid one, a cruiser is holed in its bows by a tin fish (torpedo) dropped from the starboard. Fortunately the damage is not severe, and she continues in company. In the evening a destroyer turns suddenly and comes to a stop within a few yards of us. Her back has been broken by another torpedo, but she does not sink at once. We see the feverish activity of her crew as they prepare to be taken in tow by another destroyer, already racing up to give aid.

'Another sunset sees another terrific barrage as the enemy aircraft do their best to sink more of us before dark. A torpedo bomber flying a few feet from the water in readiness to loose his fish at another destroyer receives a direct hit from this ship's guns and disappears in a vivid burst of bright red flame. Those on board who saw it cheer wildly, and someone says "that —— will sink no more ships, anyway."

'The convoy however receives no rest, the night is turned into day by the use of flares, and is disturbed by the flashes of falling bombs . . .

'But at last our work is done, a big convoy is safely delivered with light loss, whilst the enemy have lost quite a dozen of their bombing aircraft.'

Sub/Lt. J. A. Clements, R.N., who came home on compassionate leave from West Africa, owing to the state of his parents' health, writes in 1944:

'The only exciting thing that has happened to me since Malta days is a near miss from collision in a fog at sea. . . . I went for my training [as an officer] to H.M.S. *Good Hope* at Port Elizabeth [S.E. Africa] and became a commissioned officer in

LETTERS FROM THE ROYAL NAVY

February 1943. From there I went to West Africa and was at Lagos for a short time before becoming navigating officer on a mine destructor vessel, and then I was appointed 1st. Lt. of a naval barracks, housing the staff of the C.-in-C. West Africa at Freetown. . . . I am now on a trawler-sized ship attached to the examination service, Firth of Forth. This does not please me very much in these days of momentous happenings . . . but . . . I have decided to settle down and make the best of it for the time being.'

From the same – another letter (Sept.) later.
'I was lucky enough to have my fiddle with me when I went overseas. At first just a nuisance – something else to carry around – but it proved really useful at Pietermaritzburg, where it acted as a leave pass. I made the acquaintance of a really talented lady 'cellist there and also a young lady pianist. . . . We played at concerts for the troops given in the Town Hall and Hospital there. . . . In my early days at Freetown, before I had either a Padre or a piano in the barracks, I held Sunday morning Divisions, followed by a full-length church service (except that I gave a reading instead of a sermon) and my fiddle then provided the music for the hymns. . . . . I managed to get a concert party going and put on a show at Christmas of last year. I also formed a choir and conducted a Carol Service on Christmas Eve. The Admiral, with some of his staff, came to both, and after the Carol Service made a nice little speech. . . . I had to do everything myself, including the script for the concert and the copying of the words and parts for the carols, and find time for rehearsing both, which was not easy, as the Barracks was still under construction and my normal duties kept me well occupied.'

The adventures of Sergeant Mercer appear to be of an amphibious nature.
It has seemed appropriate that they should be recorded along with the naval exploits.

From Sgt. P. Mercer, 'Beach Signals Section'.
'I really am pleased to hear from you. . . . I have managed to find another interesting job, for we work in close co-operation

with commandoes and assault troops, so you can guess we have a pretty exciting time . . . the *Journals* are packed with interest for me . . . at the moment I don't seem to be short of anything unless it might be socks. I find that continual walking around in sandy water (the powers-that-be call 'em "wet landings") has an abrasive effect on the socks and holes appear in them at a faster rate than I can cope with. I was pleased to see E. Hawthorn's* address in the last *Journal* and I have written off to him.'

From Sgt. P. Mercer.
'You will no doubt be a little surprised at finding me still with an address in England, instead of being over the water. However, it is only due to an accident that I am still here. We sailed as intended, but fate took a hand and at 1.00 in the morning of "D" Day we had to abandon ship, and after a rather bad hour in the water we were eventually picked up and so gravitated to this address. Needless to say I lost everything, but as far as issue kit goes I am now "back to strength".'

This letter also is from a soldier serving on a ship.
Pte W. J. Hamilton, H.M.S. Hospital Ship.
'Many thanks for the Christmas card from the old College. . . . Whilst in England I had very little leave, no embarkation leave and have been abroad for over two and a half years. But that still doesn't absolve me from the sin of not writing. . . . When I first joined the army three and a half years ago (to give a little of my history), I went into a tank regiment . . . but after six months of that I was transferred to the R.A.M.C., where I entered my civilian occupation once more, namely a pathological laboratory assistant. I was posted to a hospital ship and have since remained in the same post to this day. . . . During our time abroad I, or rather we, have visited quite a few foreign countries, India, Palestine, Egypt, Madagascar, and practically every port of the East African coast from Durban to Suez, that is a brief précis of our travels. I think the experience has done me good, although, quite naturally I think, I have desired to return home for many months now. . . . I would like very much some books. . . . Could you possibly procure a copy of the

* Ernie, the serving-room boy. He eventually joined the Palestine Police.

Pilgrim's Progress; bookshops don't seem to have it out here. [They didn't here either, but a generous individual had given the Comforts Fund a copy, with other books, and it was immediately posted to him.] I have the address of one of the College members, serving in Poona, India . . .'

This kind of help was greatly appreciated. The man's name was not on the serving members' register. He was written to, and books, etc., sent.

XXX

LETTERS FROM EUROPEAN THEATRES OF WAR

THE two letters printed below pinpoint a new feature of modern warfare – the soldier's anxiety concerning his family, home and friends in England.

From Pte J. W. Keir, October 1940.
'Many thanks for your kind and generous letter. . . . It was about the last thing I should expect in view of the cruel and savage circumstances in which you are so bravely carrying on in London . . .

'A letter I received a week ago from one of my workmates tells its bitter tale. When I was on leave about six weeks ago I called in to see my employers. Everything was going on well, although the staff was depleted due to call-up and voluntary enlistment. Since then three of the girls have been killed, three of my workmates have been rendered homeless, and to cap it all the factory has closed (temporarily, I hope) due to lack of power. The astonishing thing about the whole dastardly business is that the writer of the letter says that despite their bitter misfortune Hitler and his wicked associates cannot destroy their morale. For the time being one can only silently salute such heroism, but the time is coming, perhaps not very far distant, when the avenging angel will destroy completely and finally this modern plague of Nazism . . .'

LETTERS FROM EUROPE

From A/C2 E. V. Bews, November 1940.

'It seems to me that we who have joined the Forces have the best of the bargain all round, no rations, no worries, and safety from air raids. Judging by all reports you have a pretty bad time at nights when the Hun gets busy, but we are quite quiet up here.* I guess we shall have to knit comforts for you pretty soon . . .'

Here are a group of letters from Bomber Command (Europle) High-spirited young men who have learnt to live dangerousy., and even seem to enjoy it!

From Sgt G. F. Hitchen, R.A.F., November 7th, 1940.

'. . . as you will see from change of address and rank since I last wrote I am now fully qualified as a wireless operator/air-gunner on conducted tours of Germany at the moment, and believe me, it is not a bad life. We are doing our best to drop two for every one they drop here, and we kid ourselves that these we do drop are far more effective from the point of view of the war, even if not from the civilian point of view.

'. . . So far, although meeting with some opposition, but only of a negligible quality, we – that is the rest of the crew and myself – have done very well for ourselves. These trips are, of course, carried out at night.'

Here is an account of a visit of H.M. King George VI to Bomber Command. It illustrates the stimulus these royal visits were to the troops.

The same feeling is manifest in a naval rating's letter during the 1914 war, when H.M. King George V paid an informal visit to the ship on which the man was serving.

From F/Sgt G. F. Hitchen, December 10th, 1940.

'No doubt you saw in the papers, and perhaps on the Gaumont British News, of the King's night with the Bomber Command. Well, that was here. I, myself, with the remainder of the crew, was introduced to him, and I can tell you I felt quite proud of myself, what with my picture in the papers and on the screen as well. We certainly gave Cologne the works afterwards.'

* Scotland.

LETTERS FROM EUROPE

From F/Sgt G. F. Hitchen, R.A.F.
'I am still at the same place. There are better places, of course – but there are also worse. At the moment I am *trying* to learn the Czech language, but don't seem able to get beyond a certain stage, when due to posting and such like, the classes fizzle out, and we must begin all over again at some later date. . . . As you may have seen in the newspapers this past two months, these fellows I am with have been doing some very good work since being down in this part of the country.

'I don't know whether you have noticed it yourself, but although everybody wishes the war to end, they have no doubts as to *which* way it will finish? Please give my regards to the College, and may it not be long before it resumes its normal routine!'

Cambery's letter (printed below) gives a cheerful account of a mixed manned force in Bomber Command in 1944.

From F/Sgt V. R. Cambery, R.A.F.
'I'm on an operational squadron in Bomber Command, and my crew is quite a mixed bag. We have three Australians, three English and a Canadian. It is good fun being with lads from parts so dispersed around the world, and conversations often prove most interesting.'

From F/Sgt Cambery, B.L.A., February.
'I've met some really grand (Dutch) people, generous and kind in spite of the terrible Christmas they have had. Unfortunately there are many pro-German ones, but then the decent folk hate these just as much or more than we do.'

From F/O V. R. Cambery.
'When I last wrote I was a F/Sgt, but as you see from my address, I have now been commissioned. . . . I am still with the same crew (a motley collection of Allied and Dominion airmen) and we have been doing all kinds of work from long-range German targets to French targets and leading daylight formations. The job is immensely interesting, and now that we have opportunities of working in co-operation with the Army, I feel much happier in my work.'

From L.A.C. Smallwood (B.L.A.) November.

'Instead of being somewhere in Holland I am now "somewhere in Belgium" again. I have visited Brussels several times and have made some very good friends there. The first time I spent an evening there was an experience I shall never forget as long as I live. The population was delirious with joy, and what with autograph and souvenir hunters we were made to feel just like film stars. Before the Government recalled all banknotes in denominations of 100 francs and over, everybody seemed to be rolling in money, and as any sort of food could be purchased in the "black market" if you had the money, you can well imagine some of the banquets to which we were invited. But what a different story the last time I was there. People are still eager to entertain us, but food is very scarce and money also scarce. They are only allowed 2,000 francs a month. Consequently the black market has been dealt a severe blow and prices have dropped considerably. . . . We are still in tents and are not looking forward to the winter with much relish. The countryside here is as flat as a pancake, and water and mud are assuming alarming proportions. I hate to think what it will be like, in, say, a month's time.'

The following two letters, written from Italy in 1944, show a marked lessening of tension. They are letters from soldiers in a confidently victorious army.

From L.A.C. R. Bristowe, R.A.F., B.L.A. December 1944.

I am still in Italy. . . . Must admit that we are very comfortable at this location. There are plenty of film and E.N.S.A. shows (trust the Yanks for that!) and it's one of the best places I have been stationed in since arriving in Italy. We have quite a bit of spare time these days, mainly due to the bad weather. I have never seen rain so consistent – even in Blighty! . . . I have made good pals with many of them (the local Italian civilians). Evenings are often spent in their homes. . . . Many of the Ities are keen on going to England after the war, they all agree that in Italy there is very little industry compared with Blighty. Even in this district I must say that a lot of the people are rather backward.'

LETTERS FROM EUROPE

From L.A.C. L. Legon, attached U.S. Army, Italy.

'Many thanks for the *Journal*, which was received and read with interest not only by myself but by a few other fellows who up to then had not heard of the College. Since moving to Italy ... socks have been in demand ... so a pair of your smart blue socks would be highly treasured.... I am now attached to the American Army – the change is novel and complete.'*

From Sgt H. Richards, C.M.F.

'When last I wrote we were in Sicily, where our experience included the interesting and active adventure of invasion. The foremost recollection of those not easily forgettable days is the continual sunshine and heat, a marked contrast to more recent months. It was rather a surprise to find the Italian peninsula could be so cold and wet, even in winter. I do not think the two winters I spent in Northern Ireland were as wet.'

The following two letters were written when the war was near its end. There are still hardships, but the goal at long last is in sight.

From Gnr L. M. Cohen, B.L.A., January.

'You mention in the *Journal* that when I was in Normandy I found the natives somewhat unfriendly. This was not to be wondered at, as for four years or so they had had no trouble at all from the Germans, then we came along and their land was devastated. Since then I have been in Belgium, Holland, Germany, and at the moment am with my battery in action against the Jerries [Germans]; we were called on at short notice to help discourage them in their sudden attack on Belgium, and already I believe they are retreating. Of course, you at home get the news much more quickly than we do, although we are on the spot.... I had studied French and German at school and at the College, and am now quite good at French, and to a lesser extent at German.'†

* In the U.S. Army the air arm is an integral part of the army organization, not a separate entity.

† The writer found he could make himself understood by both Dutch and Flemings by speaking in German very slowly.

LETTERS FROM EUROPE

From Sgt Connelly, B.L.A., December 1944.

'Had quite a nice enjoyable time over Christmas, was fortunate enough to have a roof over my head, and a real bed with white sheets to sleep in – a great luxury. The weather over Christmas has been really super – cold of course, but the sun has obliged all day for the last few days. Previous to this it has been pretty ghastly, water and mud everywhere . . . and as we were in close contact with the enemy, we had to put up with sleeping and living in dug-outs of mud most of the time. Our experiences of the people of Holland have been very mixed ones. Some folks are extremely kind and helpful, but we have had to deal with numerous pro-German ones, and collaborators.'

These next two letters are grouped together for the contrast they present. The first, from F. W. C. Watts, written in 1940, at the desperate opening of the European battle, the other from Second Lieutenant G. A. Brown, dated December 1944.

From Cpl F. W. C. Watts, R.A.M.C., writes in 1940

'. . . after two months at Dieppe we suddenly evacuated. The ambulance train was bombed and I lost all my belongings including the books sent by the (College) Work Party. I left France on a Sunday. On Wednesday when I arrived home I found that my house had been blown up by a bomb. I am pleased to say that both my mother and father, who were in the house, are well on the way to recovery. After six days at Leeds, I was posted to this C.C.S.* where it was thought maybe I ought to have a couple of stripes. All the very best wishes to the College men who are holding the fort for those serving.'

From Sec/Lt., G. A. Brown, December 1944.

'I have been over here about two months. . . . In general the Dutch are short of food; potatoes and greens being the main diet, a little meat and brown bread with butter. The main sentiment being that they would rather live humbly with us than moderately with the Germans. I spent a very pleasant Christmas. We gave a party to the local children and cheered them up with a few little titbits that the troops very gallantly forewent. The Dutch version of Father Christmas presided over the whole

* Casualty Clearing Station.

party and the thing went with quite a swing. Dances are rather difficult to arrange as the folk are strictly religious and we have to get the priest's blessing before the dance gets any girls.'

Lieutenant R. L. Locke's letter, the first to reach the Work Party from Occupied Germany, gives an account of conditions there in striking contrast to the descriptions sent from Germany by members of the occupying force in 1918–19 that appear at the end of the first part of this book.

From Lieutenant R. L. Locke.
'Very few of the civilians seem humiliated, some even try to be friendly. They certainly have been short of very little; being well clothed, and apparently well fed. They have lived on the fat of Europe for five years. Non-fraternization is very difficult. The children cheer the columns as they pass the towns and villages, and of course come round to us when we are stopped. It is so difficult to treat these little mites as one feels one ought to treat the Boche. It is so natural for our chaps to be friendly, and it is almost instinctive here to be the same. However, so far I have managed to harden my heart.'

From Cfn H. Hardy, R.E.M.E.
'I am now in Italy and can't say I am impressed by what I see when I look round; as a matter of fact it is nearly as bad as Sicily. . . . All day long we are besieged by hordes of local lads and lasses of all ages demanding "Biskwit", "Choclit", and anything else they think they may need; we have a stock answer to it all though: we tell them to ask Musso for it. . . . This morning we had the record-holder for cheek to date. A young girl aged about 20 came up to me with a very sweet smile and asked for a tin of petrol so that she could heat up her curling irons to curl her hair with. I asked if she could speak French (I speak disgraceful Italian), she said yes, so I began to tick her off. I think she was very surprised that her request was refused and is under the impression that I am no gentleman.'*

Here is a letter from Palestine. There is compassion in this letter and a sensitivity in the final description that is almost poetry. . . .

* A view that in the circumstances hardly seems surprising. We trust some units were a little kinder!

LETTERS FROM EUROPE

In September 1945, L.A.C. R. Bannister describes how, after returning to 'our old wing in Italy' a further move was ordered 'to the Middle East, actually Palestine. We spent seventy-four hours in a train, in box cars too. There was no organizing of meals, a standing joke throughout the journey was "there is a hot meal at the next stop". . . . We boarded the troopship at Taranto . . . and were surprised at the civilians on board. . . . We learned later that these civvies were Jewish refugees bound for Palestine. They had come from some of the worst of the German prison camps, including Buchenwald and Belsen . . . most of them still showed signs of their ill-treatment (after six months rest in Switzerland). We spoke to many of them during the voyage, and it was terrible to listen to their description of the treatment meted out to them by the Germans. A lot of these Jews were Germans, some had been in concentration camps long before the war. Well, it touched us deeply to see how happy they were – the promise of a new home was something no one could describe.

'That night we slipped out of the harbour bound for Haifa. It was a night I never shall forget. There were millions of stars and the lights of Taranto were glittering in the water, and the refugees were singing very softly . . . the last day aboard I heard the refugees got up before sunrise to see Palestine in the dawn . . .'

XXXI

LETTERS FROM THE MIDDLE EAST AND CENTRAL MEDITERRANEAN FORCES

FROM W. Davies, Middle East Forces, 1942.
'How is the College nowadays? . . . I would greatly appreciate some word from you, as you see by my address I am miles from England and having a great experience; although we are surrounded by sand, we are having quite a good time.'

From Sgt. W. Davies, R.A.M.C., M.E.F., April.
'I must thank you very much for the pleasant surprises I received from you and the Work Party . . . when I have finished with the books I will pass them on to the unit library. The warm weather has not really started out here yet, we will get it very hot later on. . . . Outside the depot, I have cultivated a little garden in the sand, and have all sorts of funny things growing therein, including dandelions, a geranium of pale pink, maize, aspidistras (so I'm told!), and of course, numerous cacti, quite a welcome change from the sand, as you may well imagine. The natives of this country are a peculiar people, for the majority wear long robes, rather like a nightgown, and I'm sure they sleep in them as well; they pester you in cafés with all manner of articles, from boot-laces to wrist-watches. You inquire the price and then offer half. For instance, when I was in Cairo on leave, I was interested in a certain article a native was selling; he asked

75 ptr. (roughly 15s.). I offered 30 ptr. We agreed eventually to spin a coin, 25 ptr. or 35 ptr; I won, and paid 25! (5s.). . . . You sit down for a cup of "char" and then the fun begins, a seeming never-ending stream of boys desiring to clean your shoes or sell you something! The flies in the summer are a terrible pest and at night we sleep under mosquito curtains. Fortunately we have facilities for swimming, and we get a mobile cinema show at least once a week, as well as occasional N.A.A.F.I. and other unit concert parties. Life is not so hard; when we get leave we can travel to Cairo or Alexandria and spend a pleasant seven or fourteen days. If one watches the budget carefully all is fine.'

From L.A.C. George Brown, Middle East Forces.
'Am afraid I can't contribute a flourishing article about the beauty and scenery of these parts. For twenty months now I've gaped at the same uninteresting view, totally devoid of any beauty, which is comparable with the greater part of Egypt. But why worry. It can't last for ever, and one of these days I shall once again breathe the clear fresh air of England and gaze upon the green hills.'

George Brown did return home safely, but he died comparatively young a few years after the end of the war.

From L.A.C., G. Brown (to George Bankes).
'No doubt you have heard that my parents had a post-card from young Bill telling them he is a P.O.W. in Jap hands.* Am glad to hear that the Maurice C.C. is still carrying on. . . . I haven't played much cricket this year. I found that the combination of the heat and old age was too much for me . . .'

Here is a lively letter from an officer in a frivolous mood!
From Lieut. G. Lansbury, M.E.F., April.
'We are going to rebuild our mess in the near future, so the C.O. has ordered a mess night tonight with the express intention of saving the WOGS the job of pulling it down. . . . I expect I shall be inveigled into it, I rather feel I must be getting old, so it might do me good.

* Bill Brown died a few weeks before the end of the Japanese war, still a prisoner in the hands of the Japanese.

'Next morning: Well, it was just as I feared, though I did manage to keep fairly sober. . . . We didn't really wreck the mess, someone started a battle with stirrup pumps, which developed rapidly into a water fight with fire buckets – grand fun, but oh, so wet at three o'clock in the morning. We did have one race through the walls and over the top of the mess, but after about three of the officers had fallen through the roof, they decided the casualties were going to be too high. . . . Anyhow, it was d— good fun while it lasted, and was certainly a grand opportunity to pay off a few old scores on the senior officers with a few well-placed buckets of ice-cold water. . . . My regards to all the gang.'

From L.A.C. P. W. Norris, M.E.F.
'I hardly know how to express my thanks adequately for the two parcels just received, containing books and socks. . . . It's really good to know that folks such as yourselves remember us out here, despite busy lives. . . . The Christmas show [which he was producing] is entailing a lot of work . . . it's difficult to get everyone together – still it's a job after my own heart and augurs well at the moment. I miss my old fiddle tremendously and have tried everywhere to obtain one, but they are simply unobtainable in these parts. . . . How's the old College progressing now? . . . Education seems to be an important and vital part in shaping the post-war happiness and progress of the nation, and I presume the College are taking the necessary steps to set in motion the machinery for adapting itself to new conditions and methods. I have no doubt that if we are to have a prosperous and educated nation, such colleges as ours will have to play an important and integral part in its progress . . .'

The theme of education, and the writers' anxiety that the College should be taking stock of its position and considering the role in education it must play after the war, occurs again and again in these letters from students in theatres of war all over the world.

From L.A.C. H. L. Paine, R.A.F.
'I must first of all thank you for your airgraph. . . . I am now at another station, this time truly out in the desert. The station

itself is quite good, but is entirely surrounded by sand as far as the eye can see. I was very pleased indeed to get your news of the lads out here and now at this moment we appear to be making a determined effort to finish the job, my thoughts are quite naturally with those of our chappies up there. Thank God the weather is a little cooler for battling, otherwise it is far too great a strain on the human frame. I shall certainly write to Bill (Walder) and Dick (Ramage) in S. Africa, and to Freddie (Catt) in Egypt. Like so many of the folk at home, I am simply longing to see the end of this nightmare and to get home to my wife again, but I am a little perturbed by the afterwards – where? what? and when? Still I suppose it will straighten itself out. Now that I am stationed away from what civilization Aden did possess, I am quite unable to go ahead with my social work, and in that respect I am a little disappointed.'

Sergeant F. W. C. Watts had asked the Work Party to send him the paper, the *Amateur Photographer*. Both he and his officer were keen amateur photographers, and he wanted to start a Camera Club in his unit. The magazine was duly sent and the Camera Club got away to a good start.

From Sgt F. W. C. Watts, 1943.
'Thank you so much for your letter received with a recent copy of the *Amateur Photographer* ... I would be extremely grateful if you could send them regularly.'

They were sent – the Camera Club flourished, and the magazine was passed round to all ranks, both commissioned and non-commissioned.

Later: 'Things are not quite so good out here,' he writes from hospital, ending, 'after 24 months out here everyone begins to feel absolutely dead beat' ('out here' is North Africa).

From L/Cpl F. W. Watts.
'We are still floundering amidst the desert sands far from the haunts of man ... occasionally a mobile cinema unit takes pity on us and brings to the camp a five-year-old film, and a newsreel of historic interest, but mostly we live upon ourselves. I'd

swop all Palestine, yes, and all its oranges too, for a plate of well-cooked potatoes. Apart from the Bedouins and their herds of sniffing camels, we get few visitors here, and the regiment, though a mixed assortment, has very few Londoners.'

From Bandsman G. Humfrees, R.A.M.C. Band (on service abroad).

'Many thanks for the *Journal* ... which I received when I was in Baghdad. I have travelled a great deal since I have been out here. The band and one girl form an Ensa concert party, which goes by the name of Thirty Men and a Girl, which I'm afraid is an obvious crib.* We have been touring now for about five months. So far we have played in Egypt, Palestine, Iraq, Persia and Syria.'†

From Cpl J. A. Hare, C.M.F., January.

'In some four years of overseas service I have twice visited Egypt, Libya, also the Cape, Aden, India, Ceylon, Burma, Iraq, Persia, the frontiers of Turkey, Syria, Lebanon, Palestine, the Sinai Desert, and now Italy. My thirst for travelling is momentarily appeased.'

From L.A.C. I. Woolford, March 1943.

'I was very happy to have two airgraphs from you and also a precious copy of the September–October 1942 *Journal*. ... I recently heard from A. Payne, who is now in the Army. He is well but writes wistfully of the old days. ... The books you sent me gave me (and others) hours and hours of pleasure; I appreciated them more just because I know they were sent from the College. Yes, they formed a chain linking the College and man together. ... If you have ... [follows description of other books wanted]. I enjoyed a wonderful leave last December, when I visited Luxor and Thebes and later Asswan and Upper Egypt. My memories of this experience are many, but the sight I recall most vividly is the gold-masked mummy of King Tutankhamen lying in his tomb where he has laid for over three

* The 'obvious crib' was from the title of a popular film of the day '100 Men and a Girl'.

† The College produced a bandsman in the First World War. He also travelled on tour with the band, but not to such unusual places. Cpl Hare, however, could rival Bandsman Humfrees' travels!

thousand years. I am keeping in good health and now that I have nearly completed three years overseas, am looking forward more and more to returning and being with you all again. My best wishes to you, Mr Franklin, and all members of the College and the splendid Work Party.'

From Cpl I. Woolford, R.A.F., M.E.F., November 1943.

'At the moment there is no shortage of music in the Middle East, for a great United Nations Music Festival has just commenced (November 1943). The concert of the series which I attended had Dvořák's symphony from the "New World" as the highlight – a most beautiful work. Another treat for me was a visit to this camp by the great pianist, Solomon.* He played most interesting pieces and held us all spellbound. We considered ourselves most honoured and extremely lucky! I recently took a week's leave and enjoyed a lightning tour of Palestine. Travelling up there and back was exciting, for I hitch-hiked both ways!'

From the same (dated March, written in England).

'I am sending this to thank you for your welcome airgraph and also to advise you of my return to England. I am enjoying my leave more than I can say. I was very interested to learn that Solomon had played at the College. He is a charming man.'

From Cpl F. Catt, R.A.P.C., 1942.

'At long last I have found myself an outside job as cashier.... I have landed a job I have been after for a long time. I am situated on a small island which communicates to the mainland by a causeway, so we are almost surrounded by water. The house where we are billeted serves as an office as well as sleeping quarters. However, not much of my time is spent here as I am out most of the day at camps and aboard ships. My work consists of changing all types of money into whichever currency is

---

* World-famous pianist. Started his career as a child prodigy. About 1955 he was crippled by a stroke that ended his career as a pianist. Between the wars he was persuaded by Charles Hambourg to play a concerto with the College orchestra at one of the Ladies' Night concerts. For this performance he gave the orchestra two rehearsals.

required, and making advances to officers and men. The hours as usual in this type of work are fluctuating and many times we are out on the job at four in the morning. This is generally when we go out to meet an incoming ship. It is quite a job climbing up rope ladders in a moving ship, and many is the time I have had a soaking. Recently I contacted Bill Walder and Co. From the *Journal* I shall be able to trace a few of the College men on my next leave, as from the addresses given I have been able to trace their stations. Needless to say I am very pleased to be now able to be in the show, and hope to see more of it soon.'

From the same, a later date.
'You will be very pleased to hear I have recently seen Bill Walder and Dick Ramage. The few hours we spent together were the best I have had out here. I knew Bill had received a "blighty" and was waiting for him on the quayside. He was pleased to see me. When he was safely placed in bed on the hospital ship. I went and spoke to him for a while. A tall figure loomed up and caught my arm – it was Dick. He also had a "blighty". He was amazed to see me and especially Bill. The last time they met was on the field. We were three kids together until the ship sailed. . . . Am trying very hard to get news of Ronnie Bristow and Geoff. Brown.'

From Cpl F. Catt, R.A.P.C., February 1943.
'Have been at this station for the past three months and enjoying the life very well. Have a roving job, do about 500 miles per week in a lorry, and pay the troops wherever we find them. Life is lived under the sky . . . am fit and well. Missed George Brown by a few days when I was in Cairo last October. . . . Have recently heard from Jimmy Boyce, Ron Bristow, and Geoff. Brown. All well.'

From Cpl F. Catt, C.M.F., to W. Walder.
'I am writing to you from Italy. After the end of the campaign in North Africa I had a very easy job sitting down with the 1st Armed Divn. Here I met Tom Badger. One day we were detailed to move on again and went into our Head Office some twenty miles away and changed all our cash. Saw the O.C. and

he wished us a pleasant journey. Returned to camp and commenced to pack up. Had the truck nearly loaded when an order came from H.Q. Sqdn. to wait until a messenger came from our main office. He came, and what a surprise – it was my movement order to report to base, Cairo. After seeing the O.C. only a few hours before, I could not understand it. However, I was very disappointed as I could see that it was the end of my Field days; how very much I was wrong. So I packed my kit and went back to H.Q. Here I again saw the O.C., and he told me that orders had just come through for me to return to Cairo, no explanation being given other than I was to go out of the desert after over six months up there. Transport was a staff car with a Colonel and a Major. We set off the following day and commenced our two thousand miles trip. After an hour's ride I caught half the desert in my eye. It soon began to pain, and when I tried to remove it, my eye became inflamed. I stuck it for about three days. On arrival at Base I decided to go and see a specialist. He immediately ordered me to be detained as I had contracted an ulcer on the eyeball. Well, that was a ——. Here I stayed for eight days and received treatment. At the end of this period I was completely fed up and glad to be on the move again. But what different circumstances this time, no staff car, and with that collection of kit I had, I had quite a job to get to the Transit camp at Bengazi. Have you ever been in it? Well, I was there for about five days, and still no chance of transport. Even if I managed to get aboard, it meant going down to Tobruk by wagon and then on that awful train through to Alex. So I decided to slip into Bengazi and see an Officer I knew in the R.E.M.E. What luck, he wanted a spare driver to take a wreck down the Delta, passenger being a W.O. who was proceeding to O.C.T.U.; just the job. Arranged to leave the following day. It was a Chev. that had been used by the Senusi, and it was a "wreck". Open back, canvas-covered cab and odd wheels. We commenced the trip by removing one wing, as the wheel would not turn otherwise. We intended to drive in in four days; we did it, but what a job. *En route* we had a blow-out, had all four tyres off, changed the wheels around, removed the other wing and little spots of engine trouble. Coming down Sollum pass at night the wind caught the bonnet, and that was the last of that. Can you imagine what the control posts said when they saw us coming down the road. However, I drove it into Cairo and on to Abbassia, in the four days. Following morning I went to see the Colonel, and he told me that I was posted to Base, pending another job. Gee, I thought that was my end. After a very weary week in Cairo I had given up hope until one morning the Brigadier called for me. Together with an officer, ex-W.O. who came out on draft, we were interviewed and told that we had a very special job to do. Messed around for a day or two getting equipment together and at last set off for an unknown destination – very mysterious, what! Travelled for twenty-four hours by train and landed up at a sea port. Here we hung around for a few days and eventually at midnight departed in a Destroyer. Sailed for another twenty-four hours and reached our destination. Just a small island. Had a bit of fun and landed. Here we commenced our duties and in a week we had finished our job; then waited for transport back. I may say that we travelled to our port by an Italian Destroyer manned by Greeks; had quite a pleasant time on the island except for the fact that we had very little rations. Before we left we each had a week's rations issued and when I opened mine I found that it contained fourteen bars of chocolate, biscuits, bully and tea ration, but, unfortunately, the chocolate had gone bad and ruined the contents of the box. So we took it back to the stores that had been opened. The lieutenant in charge gave me one look, and said that he would gladly change it – just go inside and pick yourself another box! Like Mother Hubbard – when I got there the store was bare. So we had half rations for a week. Water was useless, so my officer and I drank the local wines for a week. Here the population was now only aged and infirm, and what a pitiful condition they were in. Believe me when I say that I saw people sucking pebbles. The reception to us was marvellous. However, I must not say too much about this here, but will tell you all one day. An Italian seaplane was going back to Mid-east, so we scrambled in and soon we took off. Had an uneventful journey back and landed back at Alex. Train back to Cairo and placed the report before the Brigadier. He was very pleased and told me that he would soon find me another job.'

The writer had further adventures driving over almost trackless desert routes in broken down cars, but this sample must suffice.

From Cpl F. Catt, R.A.P.C., C.M.F., May 1944.
'In this ward we have Poles, French, Germans and Italians, and the noise we make is terrific. Somehow we all manage to make ourselves understood with a few words of each language, and I think I have managed to make the Jerries realize that we have won the war, and it's only a question of time. One good line of propaganda I took with them was to conduct them to the radio, and switch on Berlin for them to hear, then to compare the news they heard to London, and our local newspaper. Seemed to impress them quite a lot.'

Below is one of the many letters expressing appreciation of the link with the College that the *Journal* and the Work Party between them have helped to forge for the men in the Forces serving overseas.

From A/C1 L. A. Shaw.
'Thank you very much for the socks and copies of the *Journal*. . . . The *Journal* is really a wonderful idea for everyone keeping touch with all their old College friends. I think the *Journal* and the Work Party are doing more than anything to keep the old spirit and friendship of the College alive, when it could so easily be lost in these times, when the members are scattered in the four quarters of the globe . . .'

XXXII

LETTERS FROM AFRICA—NORTH EAST AND WEST, FROM CANADA AND FROM PRISONERS OF WAR IN GERMANY

From A. V. Bews, July 1942. Laboratory, 6th General Hospital, Kenya.

'Have now arrived in Mombasa, which is to be my permanent station.

'I am quite well and happy and am in charge in my own laboratory with two native assistants. Am hoping to be a sergeant very soon. Have loads to do and do not get much time off... would like my violin sent, complete with everything and music...'

The above was written to his mother who forwarded it to the Work Party. Books were of course sent, but I don't think he ever got his fiddle... the practical difficulties of sending it were great.

From Lieut. W. A. Catch, R.A., April 1943.

'I have been living in an atmosphere of extreme excitement and strain during the last fortnight – I think my grimmest out here, and that is no mean statement – and the arrival of delayed mail, including your letter with September–October *Journal*, was most heartening. I am of course, keenly interested in the news of College men in the Forces. . . . Incidentally, he [Mr Franklin] will be interested to know I am as extreme and unrepentant in my politico-sociological views as ever . . . it must be the Irish blood in me,* Except for some scratches I am unscathed, and my journey through N. Africa is, I hope, nearly over. . . . The list of addresses is very welcome and I'll communicate with as many as I can. Dear old Jack Lawrence, the last time I saw him was in the common-room, flanked by a fire on one side and a large pint glass (part filled) on the other. I hope you'll let my many friends in the College know by some means that I'm still disgustingly alive, and as stubborn as ever. . . . The men under my command – seventy-five of them – have been magnificent all the time in the very trying circumstances and under great hardships most of the time, and it is almost a sacred duty imposed upon us to see they get a square deal after the war is over . . .'

From Lieut. W. A. Catch, M.E.F.
'I have been a rover along the African coast, and, in fact, was a gipsy until two weeks ago, when we settled down to a special job. The change of address means a change of duties . . . and we find ourselves again living in hillside dugouts, and I have had many hours' amusement converting the inside into a replica of a country inn parlour; oak beams, wainscotting, oil lamps, and even advertisements for the local cattle show. The only things lacking are cuspidors and sawdust, but being officers and perforce temporary gentlemen, we don't notice the omission!'

From Lieut. W. A. Catch, M.E.F.
'The English Inn has now been exchanged for a ruined castle – a most interesting place, built by the Turks on foundations consisting of Greek graves – at least the Greeks founded a city near by and carved their tombs from the rocks. . . . There are ruined settlements over which the sea spray dashes, a keep, and dungeons, and a most companionable owl of the little variety, which answers when I whistle at dusk! We have already established some fowls in the courtyards and are getting a

* Catch attended Franklin's class on finance. They had many an argument together – and a mutual liking for one another. Politically, Catch's views were Communist.

regular colony of snipe on the seashore, searching for scraps. . . . We are finding Greek and Roman coins, with skulls and thigh bones from the graves, and also other remains, including cruse lamps. . . . I am, strangely enough, still very fit, getting a fair amount of reading done, and also some water-colour painting. Some eight or nine I am definitely ashamed of are going into an art show here very shortly, and some day I may have the pleasure of again putting exhibits into the College show.'

Here is a display of high spirits in North Africa!
From L/Cpl T. Badger, 1944.
'Referring to Christmas, had a slap-up time here . . . my hopes are still high [for getting home leave so as to be in London in time for the annual Old Students' Luncheon]. . . . Owing to a bad foot have been on light duty, and the last few days confined to bed. . . . Our celebrations (for Christmas) were pretty hectic, plenty of everything, also had three days holiday, so we let ourselves go.

'The New Year I saw in pretty quiet . . . supper, and a few drinks on the strength of it. . . . The wagon managed to get us back in time to hear the wireless, and have a few more drinks. My hopes were to be in bed early, but fellows were roaming round tipping them all out, so it was quite a while before I made it safely.'

From Rfn H. Hardy, B.N.A.F., 1944.
'Since last June I have been away from my old company, and went from them to an Ack-Ack unit, and went on to the Sicilian invasion with them, and stayed until their campaign finished, when I had a serious illness and came back to North Africa again by a hospital boat. Believe me, it's quite an experience having a couple of Itie prisoners of war carting me around on a stretcher, and, in fact, I should say that it was the first good piece of work they have ever done in their lives; so you can guess how much most of our lads regard them. After being discharged from "dock" my travels began again, up and down Algeria and Tunisia, in and out of transit camps, etc., until a week ago I got to a unit. . . . Contrary to ordinary beliefs, North Africa can be very cold; for the past two or three days I have lain in bed stone cold and have been praying for a pair of

bed socks; it seems that thanks to yourself and the kindness of the Work Party I am now warm again. . . . Since being out here just over a year ago I have had some fun as well as some bad moments; at one time I was i/c about 250 Arabs who worked for the old unit. I must look a mug, so I got the job of making them work, and believe it or not it's a thankless task; an Arab is born lazy . . . anyway, I managed quite well. How's things at the College these days?'

From G. H. Briancourt, British North Africa Force, 1945.
'Well, I still survive and in pretty good health, thank you. . . . The report of the November–December Council Meeting is most interesting, and it is very gratifying to read of the consideration being given to post-war policy. It almost seems as though the Council is gifted with clairvoyance, for whatever it considers, these things occupy Parliament's and the Army's attention within a few months. The Army Education Corps in my district have organized a very fine educational programme for the coming season. . . . In addition to elementary French, I have optimistically entered myself for German and arithmetic. I say "optimistically" for I doubt if my company will have enough names . . .' [i.e. to justify a class in those subjects being formed. He appears to take a poor view of his fellow soldiers, at any rate intellectually!]

From L.A.C. Penfold, Anti-Locust Flight, E. Africa Forces.
'I have been on the move again, and this trip of about 6,000 miles has proved very interesting. It was made by land, sea, and air. The sight that was most welcome on arriving in East Africa was the green fields and trees after seeing so much sand in the past. The trip by sail (eight hours) was most interesting, as we passed through plantations and jungle. We saw antelopes, ostrich, wild buffaloes, giraffe, baboons, and wild geese, also the many plantations that East Africa is noted for. During the trip one reached air altitudes of 6,000 feet, and saw bananas, pineapples, and passion fruit growing by the wayside, and this brings me to my present address, which is a very nice camp, and we get good food, which is a great asset. . . . The anti-locust flight . . . is a new experiment to try and exterminate the locust pests, that are very prevalent in this country, from the air by

means of a powder which is sprayed over them by aircraft. If this is a success, which I have very good reason to believe it will be, it will be the means of saving thousands of pounds' worth of crops each year, so you can imagine the farmers are hoping for good results.'

From L.A.C. H. V. Ridler, W.A.F.
'I am afraid the September–October number of the *Journal* must have travelled round the world before reaching me. . . . I left Orkney so suddenly that I had no time to let you know my change of address. . . . It is not really bad here [West Africa], or not as bad as some fearsome articles in the British Press have made out. The climate is more tiresome than anything else, and malaria is contracted very easily, with other more dangerous diseases a long way behind. The evenings are quite cool; but unfortunately it is always dark soon after seven, which means that you cannot take advantage of the coolness for walking. The food is dull. It could be much better; but it is left to the imaginations of the cooks, and they have none, I am afraid. As slight compensation for that, we have very good billets, made largely from mahogany planks that would be worth their weight in gold at home just now; and excellent showers and locker equipment. There is also a small library and a cinema show once a week. What seems luxury at first after an English camp is the native house-boy who cleans, or is supposed to clean, one's boots and shoes, and look after one generally. You soon realize, however, that it is almost as much trouble to see that the boy does his work properly as to do it yourself – not always, of course; but these native boys can be very exasperating. . . . I was interested to see that Mr Gill had worked in West Africa. I wonder in which colony?

(Mr Gill wrote to Ridler on his experiences in W. Africa after this letter was received.)

Letters from the R.A.F. (from Canada) and from India
Although two of the letters in this group were in fact written in England, the writers are describing tours of duty in Canada. It seemed therefore correct to include them in the letters from Canada since they certainly do not emanate from the 'home front'.

LETTERS FROM AFRICA, CANADA AND GERMANY

From E. W. Kerr, Ontario, 1944.

'I am on the ground staff of a Navigation School out here and spend most of my time writing reports, etc. The shorthand, for the first time since I took it up, has come in very handy. Most of the time we are pretty busy but at the moment I'm looking forward to Christmas; we are getting five days leave, always providing that the Japanese don't invade this part of Canada! Those out on the West Coast are not so fortunate and I believe that their leave has been cancelled...

'The Canadians are a marvellous people when it comes to hospitality, and I only hope that if any members of the Canadian Forces visit the College they will get a good reception. That at least will help to repay a tithe of the hospitality I have enjoyed since coming over here last November.

'Also, I know that this will interest you, they seem to have a truer conception of democracy than we have back home, and Officers of the Canadian Forces meet us on equal terms when we are out anywhere. The same applies to working men, after working hours they are more or less treated as equals by their employers. This, after all, is only as it should be, but in the past there has been too much class consciousness in England. Most of it is, of course, attributed to the so-called upper classes but a great deal of it can be blamed upon the lower classes and their reverence for titles, etc.'

Extract from letter from L.A.C. M. Holland, who is in Winnipeg.

'As you will see by the address on the back of this letter, I am now at an Observer School in Winnipeg, and hope to complete my training as a navigator by the end of August. One of the first things I intend to do when I arrive in England is to call at the College and thank you and the ladies of the Work Party for your kindness to me and my companions in the Services.'

From Sergt R. Unger, R.A.F., 1943.

'I thank you for the *Journal* which I look forward to so much.... Perhaps you knew I was on the pilots' course; well, I finally got my wings last October. In Canada I had a very good time, and the journey was a wonderful experience. The Canadian people were really very kind to us English lads, and

LETTERS FROM AFRICA, CANADA AND GERMANY

I am sure I have met some lifelong friends among them. Canada is itself most interesting, seeming to be a land of extreme contrasts, ranging from high magnificent mountains to low flat prairies, magnificent buildings to crude wood shacks; modern living, to the undeveloped life of the Indians. Also I had the good fortune of visiting New York for just a short while, and I was very impressed with that city. However, now I am back in England, and I am teaching flying. On my last leave I paid a short visit to the College to see the Art Exhibition and I was pleased to see such a fine and varied show. I am longing for the days when I will be able to come back to the College as a student. . . . Most of the chaps here wear their old school badge on their flying suits, and I would be very proud to wear the Working Men's College badge on mine. (A badge was duly sent.)

There is disillusion in the letter below. Its intensity seems to have blinded the writer to visual beauty.

From Sgmn Karpin. India, Command.
'Once again I must thank you for some books. . . . If you have any illusions about India, prepare to shed them now. . . . The air, contrary to the works of Louis Blomfield, and Hollywood, exudes not one odour of tropical splendour, but a thousand odours of various shades of intensity – and all of them assail the nostrils violently. . . . At present, as you are no doubt aware, there is an acute food problem here. There are numerous emaciated, swollen-bellied children to be seen everywhere, each with his food-tin – an old discarded tin – and hand outstretched in supplication. The picture of hordes of starving people rushing forward to gather the rice issued to them is a spectacle that many of us will not forget. . . . Thanks again, for sending me the *Journal*; it arrived coincidentally with your airgraph and made interesting, nostalgic reading.'

From Sgmn Karpin, S.E. Asia Command, January.
'I read with interest the idea that the College should be more than a vocational training ground. I quite agree. That was one of its biggest attractions, to my way of thinking, before the war. After all, there are numerous classes being held all over London

for purely vocational reasons. Out here things seem to be slowly gathering speed.'

Letters from Prisoners of War, 1940–44

A point of interest in these letters is the contrast they show between conditions that prevailed for prisoners of war in German hands in 1914 and in the Second World War. The prisoners in the First World War were half starved, parcels frequently failing to reach them. Sergeants Edwardes and Tonge depended largely on their Red X parcels, but at least the parcels arrived.

There is nothing in the college correspondence with prisoners of war in 1939–45 comparable to the plight of the wretched man in the earlier war, dependent for bread on Red X parcels from Denmark that failed to arrive till the bread had become mouldy. But the prisoner's need was such that he 'managed to use it!'

From Sgt J. R. Tonge (now discharged, repatriated P.O.W.).
'Delighted to receive your letter. . . . Unfortunately I did not meet any W.M.C. fellows out there [in the P.O.W. Camp] as most of the time I was in hospital attached to Stalag 9c, and that Stalag is not on your list [inquiries were made to Sgt Tonge in case he had been in the same camp as other College men and could have brought news to their people]. Thank you for your very kind message re. my M.M. I was lucky enough to be seen creating a spot of bother to the Huns, but you can believe me there are many more deserving cases than mine.'

Sgt Tonge, M.M., gave a talk to the Old Students' Club, a brief account of which is included here, with the letters from prisoners of war, as he spoke on his own experiences in that capacity. Prior to his capture he had achieved what he called 'creating a spot of bother for the Hun' at Calais, for which he was awarded the Military Medal.

George Bankes, in the chair at the Old Students' Club meeting, introduced the speaker as ex-Sergeant Tonge, late of the Queen Victoria Rifles, wounded and captured in France . . . and repatriated last year (1943).

Tonge's opening remarks, touching on a theme familiar to

LETTERS FROM AFRICA, CANADA AND GERMANY

thousands, the life of the trained soldier in England, were followed by an account of the sudden muster, journey, and arrival in France on May 22nd, 1940, of his unit, which, though motorized, had left their motor-cycles behind, and had been flung across the Channel to defend Calais. . . . So well had they carried out their mission that, of a whole Brigade, less than a hundred survived; but, the Dunkirk evacuation was made possible. . . .

'Is it,' the *Journal* reporter exclaims, 'quite impossible that Harry the King turned in his slumbers and murmured "Stick it – Gentlemen"; then slept again, knowing that his breed still lived and that England would be safe.'

Life in the German prisoner-of-war camps, as experienced by Sgt. Tonge, was another fearful ordeal. Overcrowding, dirt, poor food, confined space and boredom were enemies which claimed their casualties, but which also threw up men who fought back by resource and ingenuity, helping themselves and others to keep their self respect and sanity. One way they achieved this was to dress smarter than their guards when they were moved about, more or less forcing an inferiority complex on the Germans around them. . . . The two secondary points which stood out in Sgt Tonge's talk were the brutality of the Germans to prisoners of other nations; and the certainty and regularity with which Red Cross and home parcels and letters arrived.

From Sgt F. D. Edwards, Stalag B, Germany Kriegensfangenenlager.

'Just writing in the hope of finding the College still whole and things running as smooth as possible under the circumstances. I have not met any members yet who are prisoners, but it's a good sign. I am quite fit and in the best of spirits but I should like to hear from you soon.'

(This, of course, was a postcard and is only included here to show the man's unquenchable spirit. – Ed.)

From Sgt F. D. Edwards (P.O.W. Germany).

'Things are quite reasonable here, and we have plenty of diversion, a school, concerts, sports, etc. My College lessons in German have not been wasted.'

LETTERS FROM AFRICA, CANADA AND GERMANY

From the same, a later date.

'I was very grateful to receive your letter, and thanks a lot for College news, I was very sorry to hear of J. Waugh; [drowned at sea while serving in the Royal Navy] he will be missed quite a lot. Your suggestion on the College *Journal* is excellent, I should like the war period copies saved. My wife being in the services will you address them to [follows an address] where they will be kept till I return. I am sending you a photograph of our orchestra [unfortunately the Germans removed this!]. I am the conductor, and perhaps it will interest F. Barrett to know that I have quite a few recruits for the College after the war. What wouldn't I give for a glass of Pont's special now. We play a lot of football and include at least four professionals. Our good health and fitness to do these things is due solely to Red Cross food, and the spirit of the chaps here who have not forgotten how to smile and will never go under.'

From Sgt F. D. Edwards, Stalag XXB, Germany.

'Many thanks for your very welcome letter. We have had two or three notable days since I wrote last, and if it's possible I will try and get them described in this letter. August 2nd was our red letter day: we held a large sports meeting in the good old army style. Track events and other sports such as discus throwing. Putting the shot and jumping and basket-ball were very keenly contested. There were four teams competing, two from the privates, one corporals, and one sergeant W.O.s. Our team (the sergeants) won the day, with the corporals a close second. The trophy we won was a big statue of a lion that was purchased in the town, and it now reposes in a place of honour in our room; the lads have named it after the P.M. The day closed with an inter-team football match, when again the sergeants were victorious, and the band and pipes beat the retreat; the weather, curiously enough, was brilliant all day. This coming Sunday, the military band (of which I am a member) is going to the hospital to give the sick chaps a couple of hours' musical entertainment. Enclosed you will find a programme of the latest and best variety show in this camp. I thought this would be a good souvenir for you, it will give you some idea of the way the lads relieve the monotony of this life. You will find my name mentioned in dispatches on it (as violin in the theatre orchestra and, unless there is another of the same name in the camp, as one of the stage carpenters, and constructor of a machine designated as the "Slushton-on-Mud fire-engine"). Let's hear from you soon.'

One more letter from Sgt Edwards, showing his irrepressible high spirits, is given here, for it needs more than ordinary high spirits to maintain the lively activity displayed by Edwards.

1944.
'I am sending you a photograph taken during our last show [need one add the Germans abstracted the picture?] . . . I think the Crazy Gang would have been envious of it. . . . [i.e. the show he was putting on]. You will see the fire engine I built; it will carry two men and move on its own wheels – numerous things were seen to come from it; at the end of the show the engine collapsed and blew up – an invention that puzzled many of our lads here. . . . Our military concert party suffered a great loss when fourteen of the lads were repatriated. . . . We are going ahead to build up another. . . . I sincerely hope you had a good time over Christmas, we did! . . . Everybody is looking forward to great things this year [the letter was written in 1944], but that is a disease we suffer every New Year. We chaps that run entertainments have planned shows right up till Christmas. The lads call us cynics, but even cynics must use their imagination else there would be nothing to amuse the lads in between their dreams of peace.'

Cpl L. P. O'Donnell, P.O.W. (in German hands since St Nazaire).
'There are fourteen of us here, in a hut, quite a mixture; there's Welsh, Scotch, etc., but we have a good spirit. We have all learnt a lot of the Dominions, and of each other. We have an excellent theatre, and have produced *The Mikado*, *H.M.S. Pinafore*, *French Without Tears*, *Laburnum Grove*, and many others. We all play bridge, and many violent and amusing hours are spent. We have a gramophone and have received records which please us all.'

Prisoners in the Far East
There are two College men known to have been prisoners of

war in Japanese hands – Bill Brown and Aubrey Kent. Of Bill's experiences nothing is known, but they must have been hard, for he was young and strong and of a cheerful disposition, but he died in Japanese hands.

Of Aubrey Kent – who we learned later was in a forced labour gang on the notorious Manchurian railway, there was no news for four years. With indomitable courage his wife, who was one of the W.M.C. Work Party ladies, stoutly maintained her faith that he was still living. This couple should both be counted in the hero class. Aubrey returned in due course and rejoined the College. His wife remains an active member of the Ladies Association.

XXXIII

'THANK YOU' CONCERT AND RECEPTION TO THE LADIES OF THE WAR WORK PARTY—1946; ENVOI

Report from the College Journal

'THE old well-worn phrase "a woman's work is never done" no longer applies to the ladies of the Work Party. Their admirable job is done, and on Saturday, May 11th, 1946, College ex-Service men gathered to show their appreciation. This took the form of a concert and reception arranged for all those ladies who, for five long years, had worked so hard to send articles of comfort and words of cheer to College men in the Forces.

'This is no doubt the last time this gallant band will be referred to as the Work Party, for, as reported before, they have now been formed into the Ladies' Association. But the old title, like the tradition of Parliament, added to the enjoyment and flavour of the occasion.

'The honour of formally thanking and welcoming the Work Party on behalf of all of us who had received comforts fell to F. Glazebrook. In his speech he emphasized that it was as a result of the efforts of the Work Party that serving College men had been kept in contact with the College. No matter where serving members might be, there, in spirit, the Work Party would be also. Apart from the purely material benefits that service men enjoyed through the efforts of the Work Party, it was also responsible for the maintenance of that spiritual bond. This

'THANK YOU' CONCERT

was perhaps most important during those difficult war years. We could not really thank them enough for that valuable service.

'Glazebrook then went on to say that although he had had a fairly comfortable time in the Service – mainly in a chair – he realized that others had not fared so well. It was to those that the excellent work of the Work Party proved so vitally important and worth while. As proof of the zeal with which the ladies carried on their activities Glazebrook humorously remarked that wherever he went with his chair, the Work Party always caught up with him with their parcels of comforts.

'In order to show full appreciation of the efforts of the ladies of the Work Party the "Thank You" concert had been given, and he was sure it would be a memorable occasion for them all. Mrs Franklin, as the leader of the Party, had indeed achieved something really worth while, and to her and her indefatigable Work Party it was indeed "Thank You" in the very best sense of the words.

'The evening was divided into three well-defined and distinct parts. First came an hour's entertainment by a team of past and present students. Then came the interval, which was by no means the least important part of the evening's entertainment, for there was a grand supply of sandwiches and other snacks, tea and coffee to be consumed. Both Mr and Mrs Pont were warmly thanked for all they had done in this connection. Finally came a vaudeville show, called "Silver Stars", by a party of West End artists.

'We were very proud of that first part of the entertainment because the artists concerned showed up well against the professionals who followed. F. Pratt, a present student, gave a very enjoyable pianoforte recital – we are expecting to hear more of him; Rita Paton, W. Morgan and J. Smith each sang a group of songs; all were loudly applauded. In spite of what he referred to as his "utility conjuring tricks", H. E. F. Millar left the ladies amazed. If only they could come by so many silk handkerchiefs coupon-free by simply waving their hands in the air, or produce pounds of sausages in a similar manner! Fred Lovelle was up to his usual sparkling form and kept us holding our sides for half an hour. Surely we shall be listening to Fred broadcasting from the B.B.C. very soon.

'THANK YOU' CONCERT

'The vaudeville show which followed the interval contained such artists as Ronald Gourlay, the famous B.B.C. entertainer at the piano, Middleton Woods, entertainer from the Itma show, and Helena Millais, "Our Lizzie of the B.B.C.' Ronald Gourlay is of course the blind pianist, and has a style of entertaining at the piano which is entirely his own. Playing the piano in the normal way is not difficult enough, and so he played with his back to the instrument – a manner of playing quite new to us all. There was nothing Helena Millais could not do, from organizing the "Silver Stars", bringing up to date such songs of the past as "My Old Dutch", to playing the part of a cockney costermonger. Gerald Davies, the tenor, and Della Winsor, the soprano, gathered their fair share of the applause. Finally, after accompanying Gerald Davies and Della Winsor on the piano, Nora Brightwell took up the accordion to round off the show in a very popular manner with a medley of well-known songs.

'F. Barrett was the master of ceremonies for the evening, and to him and A. Paine, the secretary, R. Bristow and others, go our sincere thanks for a wonderfully organized party.'

Added to the above report was printed this note from the Work Party.

'We of the Work Party were most deeply moved by the wonderful display, the kind words spoken, and the warmth of the tribute devised for us. It was difficult to express thanks, the emotions were too near the surface. And at the back of everyone's mind there lurked a thought for the men who would never return to share with us the delight of this or any other College occasion.'

ENVOI

The account of 'Thank You' concert seemed a fitting conclusion to the 'Scrap Book of the College in Two Wars'. But to look on the Work Party as of first importance is to get the balance of College wartime activities quite wrong. It was the thing that, by its nature, caught the attention of members serving in the Forces, both at home and overseas. But the vital work that went on in the College over those long, hard years,

ENVOI

and ensured its future, was the quiet, resolute slogging of the Executive and Emergency Committees, running the College during the war, and steadfastly planning for its future at a time when there were some people who had almost ceased to believe that England had a future. It was the courage, persistence and far-sightedness of the men forming these bodies that had enabled the College to bridge the gap between war and peace and continue without a break as a vital, well-planned going concern, its curriculum ready, and in tune with the needs of the new post-war world, and teachers lined up to take the thirty-nine classes announced in the new programme.

Behind all this effort, the Bursar's resolute courage, his imaginative thinking and deep regard for the College are plainly discernible. With him the two successive Principals, Sir Wilfrid Greene and Sir Wilfrid Eady, the Vice-Principal Frank Gahan, and George Bankes laboured devotedly. All had heavy burdens of war work and responsibility to carry, but the claims of the College were never forgotten.

There were many others who played a considerable part in upholding the life and spirit of the College and preparing it to take its full part in the educational life of the post-war world. But these, partly through opportunity, but also through their vision and devotion, remain outstanding.

In any appraisal of the work done for the College within its walls during the Second World War, that of the Emergency Committee stands out above all else. It holds, and deserves, the first place.

For Product Safety Concerns and Information please contact our EU
representative GPSR@taylorandfrancis.com
Taylor & Francis Verlag GmbH, Kaufingerstraße 24, 80331 München, Germany

www.ingramcontent.com/pod-product-compliance
Lightning Source LLC
Chambersburg PA
CBHW070602300426
44113CB00010B/1367